New Directions for
Higher Education

Betsy O. Barefoot
Jillian L. Kinzie
Co-ed¹

D0885668

Reframing Retention Strategy for Institutional Improvement

David H. Kalsbeek
EDITOR

Number 161 • Spring 2013
Jossey-Bass
San Francisco

REFRAMING RETENTION STRATEGY FOR INSTITUTIONAL IMPROVEMENT
David H. Kalsbeek
New Directions for Higher Education, no. 161
Betsy O. Barefoot and Jillian L. Kinzie, Co-editors

Microfilm copies of issues and articles are available in 16mm and 35mm, as well as microfiche in 105mm, through University Microfilms Inc., 300 North Zeeb Road, Ann Arbor, MI 48106-1346.

NEW DIRECTIONS FOR HIGHER EDUCATION (ISSN 0271-0560, electronic ISSN 1536-0741) is part of The Jossey-Bass Higher and Adult Education Series and is published quarterly by Wiley Subscription Services, Inc., A Wiley Company, at Jossey-Bass, One Montgomery Street, Suite 1200, San Francisco, CA 94104-4594. Periodicals Postage Paid at San Francisco, California, and at additional mailing offices. POSTMASTER: Send address changes to New Directions for Higher Education, Jossey-Bass, One Montgomery Street, Suite 1200, San Francisco, CA 94104-4594.

New Directions for Higher Education is indexed in Current Index to Journals in Education (ERIC); Higher Education Abstracts.

Individual subscription rate (in USD): $89 per year US/Can/Mex, $113 rest of world; institutional subscription rate: $292 US, $332 Can/Mex, $366 rest of world. Single copy rate: $29. Electronic only–all regions: $89 individual, $292 institutional; Print & Electronic–US: $98 individual, $335 institutional; Print & Electronic–Canada/Mexico: $98 individual, $375 institutional; Print & Electronic–Rest of World: $122 individual, $409 institutional.

Editorial correspondence should be sent to the Co-editor, Betsy O. Barefoot, Gardner Institute, Box 72, Brevard, NC 28712.

Cover photograph © Digital Vision

www.josseybass.com

CONTENTS

EDITOR'S NOTES

Do we really need another publication on student retention in American higher education? When one looks at the many angles at which the current literature examines the subject, where does this volume fit in and what does it have to offer?

- Theoretical approaches to student attrition and persistence abound; there is little need for more conceptual models—so this volume doesn't attempt that, although it does build on these foundations.
- What works in terms of programs and interventions that impact student retention has been well documented; while this volume is not focused on yet again describing exemplary initiatives designed to help students persist and graduate, it does cite some practical and proven approaches.
- The critical societal need to improve student degree attainment has been made powerfully clear; although this volume doesn't add to those calls to action, it is a response to them.
- The merits in broadening the retention discussion to embrace student success and student learning have been thoroughly explored; while this volume affirms these educational outcomes, it warns how expanding the retention agenda beyond institutional rates of degree completion can distract efforts to improve these rates.
- Data summaries on rates of retention and degree completion are voluminous and accessible; this volume does not reiterate such data, but it is informed by this research.
- The growing complexity of the environmental context for retention—including the inadequate national data, the impact of poor K–12 education, shifts in federal and state policy, increasingly diverse student populations, and the swirl of students between postsecondary institutions—has already been described; although this volume acknowledges this context, it does not attempt to elaborate on these complicating factors.
- The natural variations in retention challenges and strategies across sectors of higher education institutions have been discussed; while this volume doesn't speak to the distinct and differential realities facing two-year institutions, for-profit institutions, small liberal arts colleges, and large research universities, it does attempt an ambitious argument that transcends these differences.

In the midst of the exhaustive collection of work that already exists on student retention, this volume goes in a new direction by addressing the difficulty in gaining traction at the institutional level in improving student retention and degree completion—especially at larger four-year institutions where size, complexity, and diversity of structures and processes present

NEW DIRECTIONS FOR HIGHER EDUCATION, no. 161, Spring 2013 © Wiley Periodicals, Inc.
Published online in Wiley Online Library (wileyonlinelibrary.com) • DOI:10.1002/he.20040

particular challenges. Although there is an obvious need for national, statewide, and systemwide attention to the social and economic imperatives of improving rates of degree completion and levels of postsecondary attainment, the individual institution is where the proverbial rubber meets the road, and that is the focus of this volume.

The premise is simple and grounded in Senge's (1990) admonition that organizations are what they are because of how we think about them. The way many institutions approach the retention task is hampered and hobbled by a number of traditional and prevailing inclinations, predispositions, and assumptions—or what Senge refers to as the "mental models" that dictate how we perceive the challenges we face, the problems we must fix, what we consider to be relevant information about them, and the responses that we orchestrate. This volume is about helping institutions better focus their time, energy, and resources in their retention efforts by reframing the way they think about it.

This volume is organized into two main sections. In the first section, chapter 1 introduces a framework for thinking about student retention— the 4 Ps of retention: *profile*, *progress*, *process*, and *promise*. Each of these is explored in chapters 2 through 5. The second section of this volume, chapters 6, 7, and 8, explore applications of the 4 Ps concepts by giving examples of how institutions have implemented institutional improvements that can be seen through a 4 Ps lens. Chapter 9 then argues the value that new accreditation requirements offer in getting faculty engaged in the retention effort. Chapter 10 concludes the volume by offering some themes and practical observations on using the 4 Ps framework.

The 4 Ps framework has been developed by a close group of colleagues at DePaul University charged with leading the institution's retention agenda. This book, like those institutional change efforts, has been a truly collaborative effort. The framework and this exposition of it are the result of our thinking and working together over many years. Brian Spittle, Caryn Chaden, and Carla M. Cortes have all worked diligently with me, not only on their own contributions to this volume but also to each other's and to the entirety of the work. At my request, Charles C. Schroeder and George D. Kuh brought decades of valuable experience and practical insight to this text. My own understanding of the importance of market profile stems from years of working and learning with Brian Zucker of Human Capital Research; chapter 5 on *promise* was likewise shaped by years of learning about brand marketing from Verna Donovan of Donovan Consulting, who also contributed content for the chapter. To all of these colleagues, I am most grateful not only for their commitment and contribution to this volume but also for their collegiality that constantly challenged and extended our thinking and our learning together.

NEW DIRECTIONS FOR HIGHER EDUCATION • DOI:10.1002/he

Finally, this volume would never have reached completion without the diligence of Sandra Chaplin, who has taken a cacophonous assortment of chapters and shaped them into something coherent—while also ensuring it was done well and done on time. Her many talents are reflected on each and every page and are gratefully acknowledged.

Reference

Senge, P. M. 1990. *The Fifth Discipline: The Art & Practice of the Learning Organization.* New York: Currency Doubleday.

DAVID H. KALSBEEK *is the senior vice president for the Division of Enrollment Management and Marketing at DePaul University.*

1

This chapter introduces a 4 Ps framework for student retention strategies—profile, progress, process, and promise. This framework provides a comprehensive approach to focusing retention research and strategies in ways that can improve institutional retention and completion rates.

Framing Retention for Institutional Improvement: A 4 Ps Framework

David H. Kalsbeek

There appear to be few topics in higher education so extensively examined as student retention (Seidman 2012). At the institutional level, countless strategic plans have focused on it, countless task forces and committees have convened to address it, countless statewide or systemwide reports have analyzed it, and most campuses are awash in data about it. Scholars have studied it, journals and conferences are dedicated to it, and consultancies specializing in it abound. And an ever-growing chorus of policy and legislative groups calling for greater accountability in higher education has singled out retention and completion rates as essential measures of institutional success. With the advent of the Obama administration's calls to action to increase rates of degree completion and levels of baccalaureate attainment to achieve global competitiveness, the national dialogue about retention and student success has taken on a greater intensity.

However, amid this abundance of attention and apparent richness of information, there are persistent cries at the institutional level about the scarcity of usable and actionable knowledge, understanding, or insight. There seem to be few examples of institutions that have successfully improved their overall rates of degree completion by any substantial margin. Improving graduation rates at the institutional level seems to be among the most intractable of institutional challenges in higher education.

Why is that? Peter Senge (1990) reminds us that many of the most bedeviling problems organizations face are the result of the prevailing mental models used to define and understand organizations in the first place. His work suggests that one may find the cause for this intractability at the institutional level within the prevailing perspectives and the dominant mental models that guide retention research and practice. How retention is framed and the language used to do so shape how the problem is defined,

NEW DIRECTIONS FOR HIGHER EDUCATION, no. 161, Spring 2013 © Wiley Periodicals, Inc.
Published online in Wiley Online Library (wileyonlinelibrary.com) • DOI:10.1002/he.20041

how solutions are envisioned, and how institutions respond; if those responses prove to be inadequate, perhaps it is the way the challenge was framed in the first place that is in part at fault.

A 4 Ps framework for student retention strategy is a construct for reframing the retention discussion in a way that enables institutional improvement by challenging some conventional wisdom and prevailing perspectives that have characterized retention strategy for years. It opens new possibilities for action and improvement by suggesting that institutions embrace the following concepts:

- Graduation rates are institutional attributes as much as they are institutional accomplishments and are largely a function of institutional and student *profile*.
- Insofar as degree completion is the outcome of successfully meeting the academic requirements of a curriculum, academic *progress* is at the core of retention strategy.
- Just as a rising tide lifts all boats, improving broad *processes* that affect the greatest number of students is the optimal institutional focus.
- Focusing on those student outcomes that are integrally a part of the institution's core purposes and brand *promise* brings reciprocal benefits to the institution as much as to the students.

Lessons from Typical University

A hypothetical institution, Typical University (TU), can illustrate the perspectives on retention often exhibited at colleges and universities. The precipitating problem at TU is this: Graduation rates are lower than somebody thinks they should be. That somebody may be the president, the provost, the board of trustees or regents, a strategic planning committee, or a faculty council; perhaps an external accrediting or bond-rating agency assessment precipitated the concern. Regardless, there is a charge to study and improve the institution's retention and graduation rates. In response to that charge, TU, like most institutions, has assembled a retention task force.

The retention task force at TU is most likely composed of faculty; student affairs professionals; academic administrators responsible for support services, such as advising; and some representatives of enrollment services, such as financial aid. Their perspectives on retention naturally stem from their respective roles and responsibilities at the institution, roles that are oriented to the needs of individual students and their successes and failures. It is typically a highly individualized, student-centered approach that will orient the task force to begin its work in this way:

- The TU task force will compile retention and graduation rates at peer or comparable institutions, rank those comparative institutions in terms of those rates, place TU's institutional performance in that comparative

NEW DIRECTIONS FOR HIGHER EDUCATION • DOI:10.1002/he

context, and proceed to review what institutions with higher rates are doing right and, by implication, what institutions with lower rates are doing wrong. The task force, in other words, will begin its work from a premise that institutional retention and completion rates are primarily the outcome of institutional effort and investment, reflect the efficacy of a retention strategy, and measure an institution's achievement.

- The TU task force will in all likelihood realize from its initial analysis that the bulk of its undergraduate attrition occurs in or at the end of the freshman year, and that finding would be consistent with its review of the existing literature (Seidman 2012; Tinto 2012). Task force members will then focus their attention on improving first- to second-year persistence. The TU task force will in all likelihood also engage in an extensive study of the characteristics of students who consistently demonstrate a retention or graduation rate that is far below that of the institutional average. Once that small group of "high-risk" students is defined, TU will focus attention and resources on improving the likelihood of that population's persistence.

- Finally, the TU task force will assert that "Retention and graduation rates themselves aren't the goal—it's about student success." Or perhaps, "Retention and graduation rates are the outcomes of ensuring students' academic and social integration, involvement, or engagement." The task force will draw these insights, too, from the existing literature and theoretical models (Astin 1985, 1999; Bean 1985; Kuh 2007; Tinto 1975, 1987). Its agenda will expand to embrace what at least seem to be broader and bolder objectives and aspirations. The TU task force will seek to improve student satisfaction and student learning in order to improve retention. It will then rename itself the Student Success Task Force.

These actions, taken to improve institutional retention and degree completion rates, are reflective of some of the prevailing perspectives, mental models, and core assumptions about retention widely held by higher education professionals. They likely seem familiar to anyone who has served on a campus retention committee. They are also illustrative of why TU and the institutions it exemplifies struggle to gain traction in improving the institution's degree completion rates—which was the task force's initial explicit charge.

Retention and graduation rates, like any other enrollment management goal, are broad enrollment measures to be assessed and addressed as institutional attributes and outcomes. Yet typically the retention task force at hypothetical TU does not address these rates as population metrics to be modeled, measured, and managed in the full context of other institutional metrics and enrollment dynamics; task force members have an individualized, student-centered, and interventionist orientation—not an institutional one. To use a health care analogy, TU's committee approaches its task more like nurses caring for individual patients when the challenge requires the work of epidemiologists and public health officers addressing broad, systemic population metrics. TU will likely struggle to achieve its overarching charge because it will underestimate how tightly connected retention is with other institutional attributes and enrollment dynamics. The university will overemphasize approaches to student success that are not directly determinate of degree completion, and it will attend to making improvements at the margin, rather than at the core, of institutional activity.

A 4 Ps approach—which focuses on *profile, progress, process,* and *promise*—may be helpful in reorienting TU's perspective in ways that can better ensure institutional improvement. This approach can shape how the institution takes action by reframing its core underlying assumptions and can thereby move retention strategy from the periphery to the center of institutional attention—not by calling for an elevated importance but by more intentionally connecting rates of degree completion with other core purposes and institutional agenda.

Profile

Graduation rates are institutional attributes as much as they are institutional accomplishments and are largely a function of institutional and student profile.

Using just a few variables about an institution's academic and financial profile, the retention and completion rates of any American college or university can be statistically predicted with greater accuracy than many retention committees assume. In fact, even with only one institutional characteristic—the average ACT or SAT score of the freshman class—one can account for over three-fourths of the variance in institutional graduation rates (Kalsbeek 2008; Zucker 2011). While it is difficult to predict statistically any given student's first-year retention or likelihood of graduating from that student's SAT score alone (Bowen, Chingos, and McPherson 2009; Soares 2012), it is not difficult to predict the overall six-year graduation rate of an institution's freshman class from the overall class average SAT score. And when one studies a wider array of institutional attributes for America's colleges and universities besides ACT and SAT scores, there are significant intercorrelations between attributes as varied as an institution's diversity (e.g., socioeconomic, racial and ethnic, or geographic), its tuition price and net price, its residential capacity, its financial assets per full-time student, its percent full-time versus part-time students and faculty, and so on. All of these and more, as Robert Zemsky and others (Zemsky, Shaman, and Shapiro 2001) have been arguing for years, are attributes that both define and are defined by an institution's comparative market position in the highly structured and stratified marketplace of higher education. Include graduation rates and one finds that they are also highly intercorrelated, highly predictable, and an essential measure of market position. As a result, much of the variance in institutional retention and graduation rates can be accounted for without knowing anything about the institution's investment in and execution of explicit retention practices and strategies.

The implication is that if an institution's retention and graduation rates are demonstrably tied to the institutional and student profile, these rates are as much a function of what the institution is as what it does. Granted, these enrollment outcomes can be improved with intentional investments and attention, and they can erode as a result of institutional negligence. There is indeed a considerable range of retention outcomes among colleges and universities that share similar institutional and student profiles (Astin 2005; Tinto 2012), but the strategic question to be asked at the outset is that if graduation rates are so predictable without knowing anything at all about what an institution is actually doing in its explicit retention strategies, how much of the outcome is in fact the achievement of its efforts and how much is inextricably related to the institutional and student profile? At the very least, a 4 Ps orientation binds retention and completion outcomes together closely with the balance of the institution's enrollment goals and objectives and the entirety of its enrollment management strategy.

Framing retention in the context of institutional market profile is where a strategic dialogue about effectively improving institutional retention and completion rates must begin. Embracing *profile* as the first "P" of a student retention framework grounds retention efforts in the most strategic of contexts and connects it to the entirety of the institution's strategic purposes.

Progress

Insofar as degree completion is the outcome of successfully meeting the academic requirements of a curriculum, academic progress is at the core of retention strategy.

Persistence, the percent of a given student cohort that returns to enroll at an institution for a second year, is the standard retention metric and a primary measure of success in most retention efforts. It was Cliff Adelman's (2006) research that called attention to the problematic nature of persistence as an exclusive focus for institutions seeking to improve students' degree completion. His analysis showed that there is little value in a measure of the percent of students returning for a second year without also measuring if they have made one year's worth of progress toward degree completion. In fact, persistence *without* progress may be the worst possible outcome. Yet persistence is what most institutions track and what they target. In an institution's retention research, an overriding focus on measuring persistence can actually mask the real dynamics that directly determine retention and degree completion (Kalsbeek 2008).

It has long been common knowledge in the retention community that the most significant predictor of a student's likelihood to graduate is academic success in the first year (Bowen, Chingos, and McPherson 2009) and continuous academic progress after that. Ensuring that students make satisfactory academic progress toward degree completion should be the primary focus of any retention effort. All other foci recede in importance. To the degree that improving graduation rates is the desired goal, retention is not about persistence at all; it is about progress.

Nevertheless, an unrelenting and undivided focus on academic progress is not what defines or dominates the retention strategy at many institutions. Instead of affirming the centrality of academic progress, retention strategy often shifts to focus on outcomes like student success, social and academic integration, or engagement. These concepts are drawn from theory and literature seeking to explain student outcomes and indeed are important. However, when these goals take precedence in a retention strategy, attention shifts away from graduation rates—the one clear, measurable institutional objective on the retention agenda. As the agenda expands to these other outcomes, retention strategies can lose traction and lose focus; these other outcomes become ends in their own right, with retention and completion rates being indirect correlates.

A focus on progress turns attention more directly to the structures that impede student advancement toward degree completion, focusing, for example, more on high-risk courses and curricula rather than high-risk students. Courses with high failure or withdrawal rates and curricular sequences that create obstacles to student academic success stall students' academic progress. Course redesign and curricular reengineering exemplify retention strategies that reframe the challenge from one focused on persistence to one focused on the conditions required for progress. Embracing *progress* as the second "P" of a student retention framework effectively focuses on the one measure that matters most in degree completion.

Process

Just as a rising tide lifts all boats, improving broad processes that affect the greatest number of students is the optimal institutional focus for retention strategy.

The prevailing perspective in many retention task forces centers on identifying "at-risk" students, a small population of students that statistically demonstrates a greater likelihood of attrition than the overall student body. Once that group is identified, a disproportionate share of attention and resources is typically focused on that group. This is the natural result of an orientation toward individual student outcomes versus broad institutional outcomes.

However, in response to the goal of increasing an institutional graduation rate, which is a statistical measure of the enrollment pattern of a student population, the focus should not be on statistical outliers. There is very little change in the aggregate institutional retention and completion rate stemming from even dramatic improvements in retention among small groups of distinctly atypical students.

There are, of course, many other important reasons to focus on "at-risk" groups. For example, that group may be composed primarily of low-income minority students, graduates of urban high schools, or even students in certain academic programs. Institutional values and mission-based purposes call upon retention leaders to attend more deliberately to certain populations with high attrition. However, effectively improving overall institutional retention and completion rates requires framing the approach in a way that doesn't focus solely on the most "at-risk" groups of students with exceptional outcomes, but instead focuses on improving the overall institutional outcome in aggregate.

A more strategic response gives priority attention to broad institutional processes and policies that either help or hinder *all* students' continuous enrollment. At both small and large institutions there are ample opportunities for process-related improvements, such as improving core enrollment processes related to advising, registration, billing, and financial aid as well as integrating business processes and student services to create a seamless experience for students as they register for courses, manage their financial arrangements, and navigate toward degree completion.

If the goal is to elevate institutional outcomes and do so with limited resources, the most appropriate focus is on broad institutional processes that benefit the most students, thereby addressing overall institutional outcomes rather than only outcomes for small subgroups. In all likelihood, such large-scale improvements will have the greatest impact on those who in fact are most "at risk"—students who because of their academic, socioeconomic, and demographic backgrounds are particularly vulnerable to the snags, obstacles, barriers, and fragmentations that characterize the complex environments that are today's universities. Framing and focusing the retention agenda on improving processes that benefit all remains the key to improving the overall institutional outcome. As with "progress," embracing *process* as the third "P" of a student retention framework affirms that the causes of attrition may rest more with high-risk experiences and encounters that impact the many than some inherent high-risk student attributes that characterize the few.

Promise

Focusing on those student outcomes that are integrally a part of the institution's core purposes and brand promise brings reciprocal benefits to the institution as much as to the students.

While the prevailing retention perspective seeks to increase student satisfaction and success, these outcomes typically are defined in a way that is absent an institutionally specific context or purpose. Institutional context comes from considering institutional values and purposes, focusing not only on generic student satisfaction and success but asking: "We most value student satisfaction with what?" or "We most value success in doing what?" Such questions of institutional purpose are quintessential enrollment management and marketing questions that should be part of an institutionally focused retention agenda.

Students enroll with hopes and expectations that their college will deliver every day in every way on its promise to be a certain kind of institution—one that creates a specific kind of experience that fulfills its distinct value proposition. All of this, in marketing language, constitutes the institution's "brand promise." Students' success and satisfaction with things that are connected with the institution's brand promise solidify and enhance an institution's identity in a market where it is increasingly difficult—yet increasingly essential—to define and differentiate colleges and universities from one another.

To the extent that student attrition is a function of unmet expectations, it is a function of an unrealized brand promise. What we know from the brand marketing industry is that the negative effect of unfulfilled promises is not only on the consumer's satisfaction but also on the brand itself. For example, if there are mechanical failures in Toyota automobiles, that situation does not just create dissatisfied customers, it also erodes the Toyota brand of reliability and quality, which is a far more damaging consequence. Likewise, while dissatisfied students may not persist toward degree completion, the consequences of their dissatisfaction with experiences that are most central to the institution's overarching brand aren't just borne out in student attrition; the greater and more damaging consequence is the erosion of the institutional brand and its perceived value proposition among key target audiences and markets.

Most institutional retention efforts and strategies are not framed with marketing perspectives or guided by brand research; this is likely a function of the typical collection of members of the retention task force. The vernacular of the marketing industry is usually not included (or even welcome) in retention deliberations. However, an essential interconnectedness of institutional success with student success surfaces when an institution's brand research and brand development provide the retention effort with a strategic orientation that is focused more on overarching institutional outcomes than on highly individualized student outcomes.

Framed in this way, institutional improvement requires congruence between the institution's brand promise and the reality of each student's educational experience in and out of the classroom. In this sense, retention is not about satisfaction and success abstractly defined but rather about fulfilling an institution's brand promise of a particular kind of student experience and outcome, as well as about student satisfaction and success with the distinct and valued dimensions of the institutional brand.

Embracing a commitment to realizing the institution's brand *promise* as the fourth "P" of a student retention framework cements retention strategy with marketing strategy and further integrates retention with broader institutional goals and with a comprehensive enrollment management model.

Conclusion

These 4 Ps of student retention frame a perspective that sets the retention agenda at the center of institutional attention and effort by intertwining retention with both academic progress and administrative process and by keeping the retention discussion focused on the one true outcome that matters—degree attainment. The framework does this by linking retention to an understanding of the institutional and student profile on the one hand, and then connecting retention with the institution's distinctive brand promise, identity, and purpose on the other.

References

Adelman, C. 2006. *The Toolbox Revisited: Paths to Degree Completion from High School Through College.* Washington, D.C.: U.S. Department of Education.

Astin, A. W. 1985. *Achieving Educational Excellence.* San Francisco: Jossey-Bass.

Astin, A. W. 1999. "Student Involvement: A Developmental Theory for Higher Education." *Journal of College Student Development* 40(5):518–29.

Astin, A. W. 2005. "Making Sense Out of Degree Completion Rates." *Journal of College Student Retention: Research, Theory and Practice* 7(1–2):5–17.

Bean, J. 1985. "Interaction Effects Based on Class Level in an Explanatory Model of College Student Dropout Syndrome." *American Educational Research Journal* 22:35–64.

Bowen, W. G., M. M. Chingos, and M. S. McPherson. 2009. *Crossing the Finish Line: Completing College at America's Public Universities.* Princeton, N.J.: Princeton University Press.

Kalsbeek, D. H. 2008, November. "When You Wish Upon a Czar and Other Observations on Student Retention Strategies." Paper presented at the AACRAO SEM XVIII Conference, Los Angeles.

Kuh, G. D. 2007. "Student Engagement in the First Year of College." In *Challenging and Supporting the First-Year Student: A Handbook for Improving the First Year of College,* edited by M. L. Upcraft, J. N. Gardner, and B. O. Barefoot, 86–107. San Francisco: Jossey-Bass.

Seidman, A. 2012. *College Student Retention: Formula for Student Success.* Lanham, Md.: Rowman & Littlefield Publishers, Inc.

Senge, P. M. 1990. *The Fifth Discipline: The Art & Practice of the Learning Organization.* New York: Currency Doubleday.

Soares, J. A. 2012. *SAT Wars: The Case for Test-Optional College Admissions.* New York: Teachers College Press.

Tinto, V. 1975. "Dropout from Higher Education: A Synthesis of Recent Research." *Review of Educational Research* 45(1):89–125.

Tinto, V. 1987. *Leaving College: Rethinking the Causes and Cures of Student Attrition.* Chicago: The University of Chicago Press.

Tinto, V. 2012. *Completing College: Rethinking Institutional Action.* Chicago: The University of Chicago Press.

Zemsky, R., S. Shaman, and D. B. Shapiro. 2001. *Higher Education as Competitive Enterprise: When Markets Matter,* New Directions for Institutional Research, no. 111. San Francisco: Jossey-Bass.

Zucker, B. 2011, January. "Exploring Enrollment Management Metrics in the Context of Institutional Market Position." Research paper presented at The Human Capital Research Symposium, Chicago.

DAVID H. KALSBEEK *is the senior vice president for the Division of Enrollment Management and Marketing at DePaul University.*

NEW DIRECTIONS FOR HIGHER EDUCATION • DOI:10.1002/he

2

The first "P" within a 4 Ps framework of student retention—profile—recognizes that an institution's retention and graduation rates are highly predictable, largely a function of the institutional and student profile, and are more a function of what the institution is rather than what it does.

Reframing Retention Strategy: A Focus on Profile

David H. Kalsbeek, Brian Zucker

Developing a Market-Centered Perspective

Over 35 years of retention theory and literature have acknowledged the importance of institutional and student profiles in accounting for cross-sectional differences in retention and completion rates between types of colleges and universities. For example, Tinto's (1987) earliest writings and models of student departure acknowledge the importance of institutional environments with particular characteristics and attributes in interaction with students with equally particular attributes. His more recent work (2012) reviews differences in retention and completion rates by types of institution. Bowen, Chingos, and McPherson (2009) also provide evidence on how retention and completion rates vary by type of institution.

The premise in this volume is that retention and completion are not only influenced by an institution's profile and the profile of its students, but are also determined and defined in underlying ways through market position. There is a substantial difference between simply pointing out that different kinds of institutions have different retention and completion rates and instead affirming that both the profile of entering students and the institution's completion rates are measures of something more structural and systemic, namely an institution's market position.

Of course, that market structure and an institution's position in it reflect the cumulative causation of many societal, economic, cultural, and historical forces, but it is institutional profile and market position where we suggest that institutional retention efforts should begin. As Kalsbeek and Hossler (2009) point out, enrollment management and, by extension, retention strategy should be market-centered, focusing externally on broad

New Directions for Higher Education, no. 161, Spring 2013 © Wiley Periodicals, Inc.
Published online in Wiley Online Library (wileyonlinelibrary.com) • DOI:10.1002/he.20042

market factors as the necessary context for enrollment and retention planning. In most of the theoretical literature, as well as in most institutional practice, retention is typically not framed from a market-oriented perspective. In contrast, under a 4 Ps perspective, market profile constitutes the first step in gaining institutional traction in retention strategy.

The Marketplace vis-à-vis Zemsky

Thirty years ago, Robert Zemsky and Penney Oedel published *The Structure of College Choice* (1983), an empirical exploration of the structure of the higher education marketplace. By looking at the nature of admission demand and prices charged by different colleges and universities, Zemsky and his colleagues suggested that one could define and describe American higher education as a market and that any given college's enrollment profile is, in large part, a function of its market position. In subsequent work, Zemsky and his colleagues (Zemsky, Wegner, and Massy 2005; Zemsky, Shaman, and Iannozzi 1997; Zemsky, Shaman, and Shapiro 2001) provided a scheme for sorting and segmenting the market for postsecondary education, arguing that traditional categories for classifying colleges and universities (e.g., Carnegie classifications as research or comprehensive or liberal arts colleges; classifications by type of control, such as Catholic colleges or public research universities; or classifications that hierarchically rank institutions such as *U.S. News & World Report*) are not adequate to explain or account for differences observed in many national studies regarding student outcomes, such as graduation rates or career and learning outcomes. The taxonomy developed by Zemsky, Shaman, and Iannozzi (1997) classifies and clusters both students and institutions in a market context and shows the extent to which institutional and educational outcomes are related to the nature and structure of the market for postsecondary education, a market within which colleges and universities compete with each other and students compare, consider, and choose among their higher education options and opportunities.

The well-known diagram of the higher education market by Zemsky and his colleagues (1997; see Figure 2.1) demarcates seven market segments that classify the wide variety of institutions of higher learning. What Zemsky and his colleagues deliberately seek to avoid is a hierarchical ranking of institutions in this continuum, mapping institutions instead on specific empirical measures across a horizontal array in a figurative diagram referred to as the "paper airplane" model of the shape of the higher education market.

To the left on this continuum are those few institutions with high demand and high selectivity, high list price and net price, high residential capacity, mostly full-time degree-seeking students, high academic profile, wide geographic draw, broad brand recognition, high percentage of full-time faculty, higher faculty salaries, and greater expenditures on student

Figure 2.1. The Shape of the Postsecondary Market

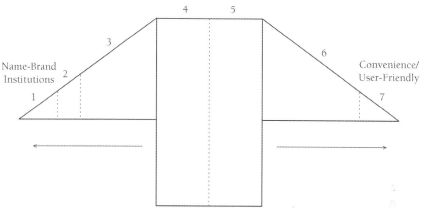

Source: Zemsky, Shaman, and Iannozzi, 1997.

instruction. These are "name-brand" and so-called "medallion" institutions, which have garnered a high level of prestige. They also have extremely high retention and graduation rates.

The right wing represents what Zemsky, Shaman, and Iannozzi call the "convenience/user-friendly" segment of the market, served by colleges and universities that teach large numbers of part-time, adult, and intermittently enrolled students who may or may not be seeking a degree; these institutions have less demand and therefore are less selective, charge a lower price, have low residential capacity, spend less on instruction, and utilize more part-time and adjunct faculty. These institutions cater to a convenience market and put a premium on offering flexibility and affordability; they also have much lower retention and graduation rates.

The middle (or the fuselage) of this depiction of the market represents the majority of institutions and the bulk of the student market. These middle-market institutions reflect a balance of two extremes; they are often in pursuit of greater name recognition, higher academic profile, higher price point, and wider geographic draw, yet need to cater to the part-time, adult, commuter, convenience market for purposes of institutional mission and financial reasons. Their students seek both the "name-brand" reputation like the institutions to the left and the convenience, accessibility, and value of those to the right. It is a market space that is highly competitive and where institutions are often conflicted in balancing market dynamics and institutional mission. It is also a segment of the market where rates of student retention and degree completion can vary widely and where the notion of "value-added" outcomes (i.e., retention rates that are higher than predicted rates) is most relevant.

This model offers a valuable way of framing a market-centered perspective on student retention. It outlines how higher education's segmented marketplace is reflected in many highly intercorrelated enrollment measures, including admission demand and selectivity, strength of academic profile, the tuition charged, the net tuition realized per full-time-equivalent student, and the diversity of the student body. Degree completion rates are squarely among these interdependent and interrelated correlates of market position.

The intercorrelations of institutional outcomes, such as retention and degree completion, have also been explored by Brian Zucker (2011), who has developed indices of institutional market position that consider institutional wealth and capitalization on the one hand and market demand and student quality on the other. His work demonstrates that more than 70 percent of the total variance in institutional six-year cohort rates across the entire spectrum of American four-year colleges and universities—public and private—can be accounted for by these two primary dimensions. When they are coupled with a small number of additional control measures related to students' socioeconomic and demographic profile, the institution's residential capacity, and its academic program mix, the level of variance explained when predicting cohort graduation rates rises to just under 90 percent.

Given the fundamental intercorrelations between institutional profile and completion rates, retention and degree outcomes at an institutional level are among the most predictable of all institutional metrics and operating characteristics. While there is a well-documented body of literature on the relatively small amount of variance that can be explained when predicting an individual student's likelihood of graduation (Bowen, Chingos, and McPherson 2009; Geiser and Santelices 2007; Soares 2012), *institutional* rates of degree completion, in contrast, can be predicted with great accuracy purely on the basis of institutional profile and position.

This observation is not to suggest in a fatalistic sense that retention and completion rates are wholly predetermined by the institutional profile. Rather, the implication, to the contrary, is that institutional retention efforts should begin by first establishing goals and objectives in a context meaningfully framed by the entirety of each institution's own distinct and definable market position. As Senge (1990) has noted in discussing necessary ingredients for systemic change, an accurate sense of an organization's current reality is just as important for a successful change effort as having a shared and compelling vision of the future. A market-centered perspective provides that essential context to understanding an institution's current reality and thereby provides an empowering mooring that many institutional retention goals and efforts fail to realize.

The analyses by Zemsky, Shaman, and Shapiro (2001) and Zucker (2011) present a starting assumption for developing an institutional strategy: that retention and completion rates are so inextricably intertwined with all other factors defining each institution's place in the stratified, segmented higher education marketplace, that they, in fact, are more of an *attribute* of the institution's market profile and position than they are an *achievement* of their various academic and student affairs activities and interventions. Attempting to frame and focus institutional retention strategy independent of a market-centered context contributes to misaligned expectations and marginalizes the essential coordination of efforts required for retention strategies to gain meaningful traction.

Institutional Interdependencies

The analyses and models by Zemsky, Shaman, and Shapiro (2001) and Zucker (2011), therefore, have important implications for those charged with leading retention efforts at the institutional level. As noted earlier, an institution's enrollment goals and aspirations—including retention and completion rates—cannot be framed independently of the market context within which the institution exists. That market context isn't an abstract concept, but rather an empirically measurable, systemic, and structured segmentation that defines the parameters of each institution's strategic situation. For example, in Zucker's construct, an institution like DePaul University that is at the 70th percentile of all private universities in academic profile and at the 61st percentile in financial capitalization occupies a market position that has a 75 percent likelihood of graduating between 65 percent and 78 percent of its freshman cohorts in six years. That level of predictability and the range of probable outcomes become the starting point for retention planning and evaluation.

That market context ties together into one cohesive fabric all of the institution's enrollment goals and illustrates how those goals are not only demonstrably interconnected but very often in conflict with each other. For example, any push for enhancing market profile by improving certain measures of student quality (e.g., via greater selectivity or higher SAT scores) is immediately in tension with goals such as providing greater access and diversity for underrepresented and socioeconomically disadvantaged populations. Likewise, goals for improving the academic profile of the student population beyond what the institution currently attracts will conflict with goals for increasing net tuition revenue if the approach to enrolling higher profile students entails more deeply discounted tuition packages to targeted student populations. These are not just tensions in concept; these goals and the metrics used to track them *de facto* tug against each other at virtually all institutions.

So, too, with retention goals and retention planning. Since retention and completion goals are interrelated in empirically demonstrable ways with diversity, quality, and access (Bowen, Chingos, and McPherson 2009; Zucker 2011), they cannot be pursued independently of these other central enrollment goals. Tradeoffs and tensions between and among enrollment goals exist at all institutions. They create a complex context where retention goals and expectations must empirically and strategically be established in concert with all institutional intentions and institutional constraints since they are interdependent, either mutually reinforcing or at cross purposes one with another.

There is a common refrain that "retention is an institution-wide responsibility" and that every faculty and staff member has a role to play in improving completion rates. A market-centered orientation affirms that retention indeed requires an institution-wide commitment, but from a different rationale. The reason why improving institutional retention and completion rates is a campuswide responsibility is not just because every faculty and staff member has an overt responsibility for and influence on student persistence, but rather because improving retention and completion measures inevitably tugs on (and often competes with) other institutional goals, values, and constraints. Because retention outcomes at most institutions cannot be advanced independently of other institutional academic, enrollment, and mission-based goals and strategic objectives, it does require a campuswide commitment to move the retention agenda forward, even if only by making more transparent or explicit how each of the distinct parts of the enterprise relate to the enrollment flow of students.

Enrollment Management

Balancing the tradeoffs and tensions that arise from interdependent enrollment goals is a defining characteristic of the field of enrollment management (EM) (Kalsbeek and Hossler 2009; Zucker and Kalsbeek 2010). EM is an approach to shaping enrollment outcomes that has become a prominent fixture in American higher education since its advent more than 30 years ago and continues to evolve both in perspective and practice. A profile perspective on how the market context creates a single tapestry of interwoven enrollment measures and objectives affirms the inseparability of retention from an institution's EM strategy.

Interestingly, nearly every definition of EM explicitly includes the importance of retention as a necessary element (Kalsbeek and Hossler 2009), and a core principle of EM is to focus equally on retention and recruitment outcomes. However, in the retention literature and models, there are few (if any) explicit references to the importance or even relevance of EM strategy and practice. Three of the most recent and important texts on student degree completion ignore the emergence of EM perspectives and approaches in higher education. Tinto's work, including his latest book on institutional effectiveness in retention (2012); Habley, Bloom, and Robbins's (2012) survey of strategies for improving student retention; and Bowen, Chingos, and McPherson's (2009) analysis of retention outcomes at the national level all make only oblique reference, at most, to EM.

For example, Tinto (2012, 17) writes:

> Enrollment management can also influence student retention by helping to shape the character of the entering class, and indirectly by influencing freshmen's

expectations of the setting into which they will enter. These pre-entry expectations serve as the initial lens through which students see and in turn judge the
institution. . . .

This statement is true enough, yet suggests that the author simply
equates EM with student recruitment rather than a broader, comprehensive
approach to pursuing an institution's enrollment goals (Kalsbeek and
Zucker 2012).

Perhaps this disconnect explains the difficulty at most institutions in
realizing lasting gains in retention and completion rates. EM, by definition
and in practice, achieves enrollment outcomes through the intentional integration of institutional policies, organizational competencies, and professional practices in concert with student-centered objectives; retention
strategy requires exactly that, yet is often disconnected from the EM effort
and organization, often centered in student affairs or aligned with academic
support services—areas that tend to have entirely different orientations to
these goals (Kalsbeek 2007).

Here are three examples of how EM, grounded in a profile-centered
perspective, connects retention with other powerful, strategic dynamics
that shape enrollment outcomes.

Admission. Admission processes are at the core of a profile-centered
perspective since for most institutions there is no clearer reflection of market position than the qualities of its applicant demand and new student
enrollment. Yet it is not uncommon for retention committees to "bracket
off" admission strategies entirely from the retention agenda. Sometimes this
is done to avoid a dead end often created by faculty saying, "If we only
enrolled better students, we'd have no retention problem"; other times it is
done because many institutions, given their market position, are not sufficiently selective to be able to substantially alter their entering student
profile.

The retention literature certainly acknowledges the importance of academic preparation in accounting for student attrition. Habley, Bloom, and
Robbins (2012), Tinto (2012), and Bowen, Chingos, and McPherson
(2009) explore factors related to students' academic preparation for college-
level academic success as an ingredient in both the retention agenda and in
the large numbers of interventionist strategies (Habley, Bloom, and Robbins
2012; Seidman 2012) that exist as ways of accommodating underprepared
students. However, few writers are as explicit as William Ihlanfeldt (1985).
Ihlanfeldt argued for the strategic inseparability of recruitment and admission from retention strategy in one of the earliest volumes on student retention authored almost 30 years ago by Lee Noel, Randi Levitz, and Diana
Saluri (1985).

A 4 Ps perspective suggests, as Ihlanfeldt did, that because an institution's admitted student profile and retention/completion rates are intertwined, admission strategies cannot be separated from retention strategies.

First, the profile of those admitted is proscribed by an institution's market position as are its retention rates. Therefore, market position is a common denominator for both admission and retention. Second, in designing retention strategies, institutions need not and should not ignore the impact of the admission process and just "play the hand they're dealt." There are significant opportunities for integrating admission and retention strategies, especially by focusing admission more on factors that are known to be predictive of student progress than on student attributes such as standardized test scores (Cortes and Kalsbeek 2012; Sedlacek 2004; Soares 2012; Sternberg 2010); chapter 6 in this volume by Carla M. Cortes explores some of these approaches. For many institutions, opportunity exists for building a more complete, enriched definition of the desired student profile that maps directly to likely performance, progress, programmatic support, and completion outcomes, although these efforts typically are at odds with the many other expectations institutions have of their admission process.

Financial Aid. The place of financial aid in any enrollment strategy is dependent upon the same market dynamics as every other enrollment outcome; the Zemsky, Shaman, and Shapiro (2001) and Zucker (2011) analyses each show that the socioeconomic profile of students, the institution's pricing and cost structures, and aid allocations are all interdependent with institutional market position. Pricing and aid, therefore, are critical and interrelated elements of a profile-based retention strategy.

Clearly, the increasing cost of a college education is contributing to the disparities in college completion rates based upon student and family financial situations (Bowen, Chingos, and McPherson 2009). While it is generally acknowledged that affordability and aid impact retention and completion outcomes, most analyses look broadly at the positive impact on retention of grant aid or student employment, or the negative impact of high unmet need or excessive borrowing, and so on. Most, however, ignore the potential of developing a retention-oriented financial aid packaging regimen that is managed as an integrated part of an overall institutional EM strategy toward pricing, aid, and net revenue optimization. Neither Tinto (2012) nor Habley, Bloom, and Robbins (2012) sufficiently address the impact that financial aid packaging strategies at the institutional level have on both retention and degree completion. All too rare in the retention literature are acknowledgments, such as those made by Edward St. John and his colleagues (St. John, Alberto, and Amaury 2000), that there are direct effects of financial aid and family financial factors that need to be included in any analysis seeking to understand the reasons for student attrition. Rarer still are arguments such as that offered by Martin (1985, 208) nearly 30 years ago that "packaging of student aid resources is one of the most fundamental yet essential tasks . . . at any school concerned with improving retention."

Today, in EM theory and practice, it is widely recognized that financial aid constitutes a powerful lever for achieving enrollment outcomes such as access, diversity, mix, quality, and net revenue, with many institutions today becoming perhaps too reliant on price manipulation through tuition discounting alone. Under an integrated EM perspective, however, that price/discount lever is not simply the level of aid or the reduction of unmet need, but the composition of the aid resources themselves—the distinct mix of student employment, loans, and grants—that are all integrated with a student's particular academic and career objectives and plans. An EM perspective views all of these outcomes—including retention—as part of one integrated and holistic enrollment strategy. Unfortunately, most institutions' enrollment and financial aid strategies place highest priority on first-year enrollments and net revenue; seldom is the optimization of net tuition revenue over the expected life of a student's enrollment even estimated, or much less embraced, strategically. The fact that there is little attention to how pricing and financial aid strategies can be designed to elevate retention and completion rates is a reflection of how many institutions are failing to incorporate retention outcomes as part of their broader EM strategy.

Absent a truly integrated approach, the isolated manipulation of single parameters to enhance retention seldom constitutes lasting solutions. For instance, for a majority of institutions, simply providing more financial aid or reducing students' unmet financial need by itself fails to produce appreciable gains in institutional retention rates commensurate with the lost net tuition revenue stemming from increased institutional aid (Kalsbeek and Associates 2009). Therefore, financial aid strategies at the institutional level require the holistic, profile-centered, enrollment-flow approach characteristic of EM strategies in order to integrate retention with the institution's financial aid, pricing, and net revenue goals.

Diversity. There is a rich literature on the particular challenges institutions face in improving retention and completion rates for underrepresented minorities, low-income students, first-generation students, etc. (Bowen, Chingos, and McPherson 2009; Seidman 2007; Tinto 2012). Institutions seeking to close gaps in retention and completion for certain populations must be mindful of the interrelationships between diversity and access on the one hand and institutional completion rates on the other. There is an increasing awareness from groups as disparate as The Education Trust, the Higher Education Research Institute, and the *U.S. News & World Report* rankings that retention and completion rates can be predicted from the institutional profile; that for many complex reasons the greater the institution's socioeconomic and racial/ethnic diversity, the lower the rates of degree completion; and that credit should be given to institutions that demonstrate outcomes that exceed predicted rates given their student profile. Yet at the institutional level, independent variables representing ethnicity and socioeconomic status often do not even survive as predictors of success in the presence of academic and non-cognitive factors for which demographic variables may be surrogates. A profile-centered strategy helps put these differences in completion rates in fuller context and frames strategically and empirically the discussion of the disparities in outcomes between groups of students and how best to address them at the institutional level.

Conclusion

The retention agenda at many institutions focuses primarily on the internal challenges and opportunities to improve institutional rates of retention and completion. Few colleges and universities begin by looking externally at how the broader market context frames those outcomes and goals. An institution's market profile, and in particular its student profile, determines in very real ways the range of retention outcomes it can hope to achieve and cements them firmly in tandem and in balance with its goals for diversity, access, quality, revenue, geographic draw, and student and program mix. Keeping these tensions and tradeoffs in the forefront of retention planning embodies a profile-centered EM perspective. Only in this context can retention efforts gain the sort of lasting traction that comes from being inseparably intertwined with the institution's entire enrollment strategy and the market realities that underlie them.

References

Bowen, W. G., M. M. Chingos, and M. S. McPherson. 2009. *Crossing the Finish Line: Completing College at America's Public Universities.* Princeton, N.J.: Princeton University Press.

Cortes, C., and D. H. Kalsbeek. 2012, October. "Innovative Approaches to Admission and Retention: Linking Admission Strategies to Student Retention." Paper presented at the CSRDE National Symposium on Student Retention, New Orleans.

Geiser, S., and M. Santelices. 2007. *Validity of High School Grades in Predicting Student Success Beyond the Freshman Year: High School Record vs. Standardized Tests as Indicators of Four-Year College Outcomes.* Berkeley: Center for Studies in Higher Education, University of California.

Habley, W. R., J. L. Bloom, and S. Robbins. 2012. *Increasing Persistence.* San Francisco: Jossey-Bass.

Ihlanfeldt, W. 1985. "Admissions." In *Increasing Student Retention,* edited by L. Noel, R. Levitz, and D. Saluri, 183–202. San Francisco: Jossey-Bass.

Kalsbeek, D. H. 2007. "Reflections on Strategic Enrollment Management Structures and Strategies." *College and University Journal* 82(3):3–9.

Kalsbeek, D. H., and Associates. 2009, May. "Undergraduate Retention and Degree Completion: Exploring the Relationship of Academic Preparation, Performance and Progress, with Financial Need and Financial Aid on Retention and Degree Completion." Paper presented to the DePaul University Board of Trustees, Chicago.

Kalsbeek, D. H., and D. Hossler. 2009. "Enrollment Management: A Market-Centered Perspective." *College and University Journal* 84(3):3–11.

Kalsbeek, D. H., and B. Zucker. 2012, November. "Toward Sustainable Institutional Strategy: Tensegrity in Enrollment Management." Paper presented at the AACRAO Strategic Enrollment Management Conference, Orlando.

Martin, A. D. 1985. "Financial Aid." In *Increasing Student Retention,* edited by L. Noel, R. Levitz, and D. Saluri, 203–20. San Francisco: Jossey-Bass.

Noel, L., R. Levitz, and D. Saluri. 1985. *Increasing Student Retention.* San Francisco: Jossey-Bass.

Sedlacek, W. E. 2004. *Beyond the Big Test: Noncognitive Assessment in Higher Education.* San Francisco: Jossey-Bass.

Seidman, A. 2007. *Minority Student Retention: The Best of the Journal of College Student Retention: Research, Theory & Practice.* Amityville, N.Y.: Baywood Publishing Co.

Seidman, A. 2012. *College Student Retention: Formula for Student Success.* Lanham, Md.: Rowman & Littlefield Publishers, Inc.

Senge, P. M. 1990. *The Fifth Discipline: The Art & Practice of the Learning Organization.* New York: Currency Doubleday.

Soares, J. A. 2012. *SAT Wars: The Case for Test-Optional Admissions.* New York: Teachers College Press, Columbia University.

St. John, E. P., F. Alberto, and N. Amaury. 2000. "Economic Influences on Persistence Reconsidered: How Can Finance Research Inform the Reconceptualization of Persistence Models?" In *Reworking the Student Departure Puzzle: New Theory and Research on College Student Retention,* edited by J. M. Braxton, 29–47. Nashville: Vanderbilt University Press.

Sternberg, R. 2010. *College Admissions for the 21st Century.* Cambridge, MA: Harvard University Press.

Tinto, V. 1987. *Leaving College: Rethinking the Causes and Cures of Student Attrition.* Chicago: The University of Chicago Press.

Tinto, V. 2012. *Completing College: Rethinking Institutional Action.* Chicago: The University of Chicago Press.

Zemsky, R., and P. Oedel. 1983. *The Structure of College Choice.* New York: College Entrance Examination Board.

Zemsky, R., S. Shaman, and M. Iannozzi. 1997. "In Search of a Strategic Perspective: A Tool for Mapping the Market in Post-Secondary Education." *Change* 29(6):23–38.

Zemsky, R., S. Shaman, and D. B. Shapiro. 2001. *Higher Education as Competitive Enterprise: When Markets Matter,* New Directions for Institutional Research, no. 111. San Francisco: Jossey-Bass.

Zemsky, R., G. R. Wegner, and W. F. Massy. 2005. *Remaking the American University: Market-Smart and Mission-Centered.* Piscataway, N.J.: Rutgers University Press.

Zucker, B. 2011, January. "Exploring Enrollment Management Metrics in the Context of Institutional Market Position." Research paper presented at Human Capital Research Symposium, Chicago.

Zucker, B., and D. H. Kalsbeek. 2010, April. "Access to Success: Towards an Enrollment Management Perspective on Educational Opportunity." Paper presented at The Education Trust Access to Success Meeting, Washington, D.C.

DAVID H. KALSBEEK *is the senior vice president for the Division of Enrollment Management and Marketing at DePaul University.*

BRIAN ZUCKER *is the president and founder of Human Capital Research Corporation.*

3

The second "P" within a 4 Ps framework of student retention—progress—focuses on ensuring that students are making satisfactory academic progress, rather than just persisting, toward degree completion.

Reframing Retention Strategy: A Focus on Progress

Brian Spittle

From Persistence to Progress

Few words have dominated the vocabulary of college retention as has the word "persistence." It gained early currency with the foundational student departure studies of Spady (1970), Bean (1980), Astin (1975, 1985), Tinto (1987), and others and has become all but ubiquitous since then. As countless book and article titles testify, it continues to shape a tradition of research and action that has taught us much about the complex relationships between student and institutional characteristics, aspirations, experiences, and outcomes.

However, many institutions still struggle to engage faculty and administrators in building campuswide retention efforts, to find the organizational levers that translate the abstractions and complexities of retention theory into scalable and durable initiatives, and to demonstrate the effectiveness of those initiatives in terms of outcomes in general and degree completion in particular. Indeed, one of the core arguments of this book is that a 4 Ps perspective helps direct institutional attention to such challenges.

It may be that the concept of persistence itself is part of the problem. Certainly, it has informed much good work on college campuses. But in directing its focus on what is the most visible marker of student retention—showing up from year to year—it has helped to shape a tradition of research that tends more to the descriptive than the analytical and has directed attention more toward interventions to minimize student departure than the policies and structures that might hinder or facilitate student success and degree completion.

NEW DIRECTIONS FOR HIGHER EDUCATION, no. 161, Spring 2013 © Wiley Periodicals, Inc.
Published online in Wiley Online Library (wileyonlinelibrary.com) • DOI:10.1002/he.20043

There are at least three reasons that explain the paradox of the persistence of "persistence" on the one hand and its lack of institutional traction on the other. First, while it makes perfect sense for campus retention efforts to begin with the data, the two most readily available sources tend to be from transactional processes, such as admission and registration, or required reporting, such as submissions to the Integrated Postsecondary Education Data System (IPEDS). While both are useful starting points, their capacity to frame retention issues or patterns in terms other than conventional year-to-year enrollment or to provoke deeper questions about which we really need answers is limited.

Second, the term persistence has always been embedded in a wider conceptual model that places considerable emphasis on integrating students into campus culture and community while paying comparatively little attention to core academic policies, structures, and practices. Presumably this was because they were either taken for granted or thought to be too difficult to modify, or yet again because their effects on student retention were thought to be marginal. In drawing on Durkheim's (1951) sociology of suicide and Van Gennep's (1960) anthropology of rites of passage for conceptual support, early retention theory tended to place greater emphasis on institutional culture than institutional structure. Culture is very important, of course, but it is also difficult to change. In any case, as Tierney (1999) has argued, the notion of integrating students into a dominant institutional culture has become increasingly problematic. For Tierney, student success in a diverse educational environment requires cultural *integrity* rather than assimilation. To this extent, retention strategies will need to go beyond models of student integration and embrace agendas for institutional reinterpretation and restructuring.

Third, the relative avoidance of core academic functions or structures has been exacerbated by a widespread tendency on behalf of institutions to see retention in largely programmatic rather than strategic terms. As Tinto (2005, 2012) has pointed out, much of the early responsibility for retention efforts was placed in the hands of student affairs professionals. Activities were often designed to tackle discrete issues and rarely involved faculty in a substantive way. As a result, they tended to be "appended to, rather than integrated within, the mainstream of institutional academic life" (Tinto 2005, 2–3). Frequently particularistic in focus and programmatic in design, retention activities were always more likely to operate within conventional definitions of the situation rather than build the analytic capacity to think beyond it.

Perhaps the notion of persistence was more appropriate to a time when speakers at college orientation programs still asked freshmen to look at the students sitting on either side of them and ponder the likelihood that one or possibly both of them would soon be gone. It was certainly a telling metaphor. Think of the synonyms: endurance, grit, steadfastness, and an obstinate determination to persevere against the odds. Viewed in this way, the educational process becomes something to be adapted to rather than embraced—an obstacle rather than an opportunity.

In their recent book, *Increasing Persistence*, Habley, Bloom, and Robbins (2012) note that the language of student retention has become more positive over time. Yet as the title makes clear, the term endures. Perhaps it is simply too ingrained in our language to be seriously challenged or replaced. For example, the authors recognize that the concept of "progression" has often been overlooked in the literature (10), but they seem to view progression in operational rather than conceptual terms. By contrast, the focus of a 4 Ps framework is less about definitions than the larger mental models that inform them.

In fact, the notion of progress has already entered the language of higher education policy. The critique of college remediation in certain policy circles and the moves to tie financial aid at both the federal and state levels to degree completion timelines are obvious illustrations. The adoption by a majority of states of prekindergarten to grade-20 alignment initiatives is another. On one level, unfortunately, the term has become associated with a narrow accountability agenda. In some expressions it does not give ample recognition to the fact that for students from the poorest communities and weakest schools, participation in any form of postsecondary education is no small achievement, and arbitrary progress indicators and requirements might turn into barriers. Yet the essential meaning of the term is both more generous and more purposeful.

Once again, the language itself is telling. Simply compare the dictionary definitions for "persistence" and "progress"—doggedness and endurance on the one hand versus movement, growth, and development (if only we could also assume the additional British usage of a stately procession) on the other—and the potential for reframing institutional thinking and action starts to suggest itself.

Clifford Adelman and "Structures of Opportunity"

The conceptual and linguistic building blocks of a progress-centered perspective are to be found in the work of Clifford Adelman, particularly his seminal work, *Answers in the Toolbox* (1999), and the subsequent *The Toolbox Revisited* (2006). Drawing on the curriculum process studies of Karl Alexander and his colleagues (Alexander, Cook, and McDill 1978), Adelman laid out a persuasive narrative—or *story* as he would put it— about what makes a difference when it comes to college completion; and it is completion, not just access or persistence, that he is interested in.

It is a story because it takes place over time. For Adelman (1999, 2006), it begins in high school; although like Alexander before him, he acknowledges that it actually starts much earlier than that. It also has a plot or at least a "trajectory." But it is not quite the retention story with which we are familiar. Adelman has little to say about the abstractions of retention theory on the one hand or the minor industry of small-scale empirical analyses on the other. Rather, his emphasis is on "academic resources" (curriculum and student performance) as the key drivers of student outcomes in college. It is an emphasis, by extension, that pays more attention to institutional structure than to culture.

Adelman (1999, 2006) is a statistician with a flair for the discursive. There is both a precision and elusiveness about his writing that may account for the impression that he is more liberally quoted than read. It may also be that what he has to say does not speak directly to the professionalized retention constituency on college campuses with its focus on the diagnostics of student risk, intervention, and support. If we are serious about degree completion, he argues, then bigger gains will be made elsewhere.

But where? Adelman (1999, 2006) encourages institutions to keep their eyes on the prize—degree completion—by focusing attention on the key levers at their disposal that enhance academic performance, continuous attendance patterns, and navigation toward degree. He recognizes the complexities of student background, motivation, and choice, which are largely beyond institutional understanding and control. At the same time, colleges and universities are what they are; there are policies, expectations, and structures that are bound to run up against student needs and preferences from time to time. Rather, Adelman directs us to the "structures of opportunity" that characterize the intersections of institutional arrangements and student behavior. It is at such intersections, he argues, that the greatest potential for institutional action resides.

At least three areas suggest themselves. The first has to do with the academic profile of entering students and the admission decisions that shape it. Even a cursory reading of Adelman (1999, 2006) would suggest that greater weight be given to the intensity of the applicants' curricula and the quality of their demonstrated effort than to standardized test scores and other more marginal measures. Surveys of admissions directors (Clinedinst, Hurley, and Hawkins 2011) consistently show that this is indeed the case in most institutions, and yet conventional wisdom and the pressure to maintain or advance reputation through other indicators of class profile may pull in a different direction.

Of course, the opportunity to take advantage of advanced coursework in high school is far from equally distributed. When such opportunities exist, though, they can be particularly powerful. Adelman's (1999) point about the disproportionate effect of advanced mathematics enrollment during high school on college completion (not just admission) for African-American students should be more clearly acknowledged in admission decision-making than it probably is.

Yet it is not just a question of mathematics. As recent research from the Consortium on Chicago School Research has shown, participation in advanced coursework in other subjects also can have what Adelman (1999) would call a "high octane" effect. Students from low-income, minority, and first-generation college families enrolled in International Baccalaureate (IB) programs in Chicago's public neighborhood schools are eclipsing other students in college admission, academic performance, and retention (Coca et al. 2012). Why IB students are doing so well clearly speaks to Adelman's point about the quality and intensity of the academic experience. It also speaks to the sorts of "profile" considerations outlined in chapter 6 of this volume and the extent to which particular environments can either constrain or open up opportunity. What is noticeable about the IB students in Chicago's public schools is not just that they are better prepared academically than their peers, but that they have gained the broader academic mind-sets for college success, such as an academic confidence, organizational and help-seeking skills, and a strong identity. Counter to what much of the research on low-income and first-generation students suggests, IB students in Chicago are well prepared for college and know it.

The second area of focus should be on monitoring and influencing the ways in which students navigate curriculum pathways so as to optimize achievement and progression to degree. The development of online degree audit systems is an obvious and important step forward in helping students and advisors do this. Paying close attention to what is happening in remedial and gateway courses is another key area for attention. As Carol Twigg (2005) has shown, first-year course redesign efforts from institutions as varied as the University of New Mexico, Riverside Community College, and the University at Buffalo–State University of New York can have deep and broad institutional effects because they are intended to increase learning, improve progress to the second year, and operate on a large scale. They can also involve significant cost savings and are, in any case, likely to be more effective than the multiplicity of add-on or parallel programs that are often disconnected not only from the rhythms of everyday student experience but also from each other.

The third (and closely related) area of institutional focus and leverage has to do with the policies and arrangements to facilitate what Adelman (2006) calls "credit momentum." As the *Toolbox Revisited* research showed, those who achieved bachelor's degrees had already accumulated more credits than those who did not by the end of their freshman year. Much of this can be explained, obviously enough, by attendance and course completion patterns. Interrupted enrollment and part-time enrollment are major predictors of non-completion, as are withdrawing from and repeating courses. There may be good arguments for generous course repeat policies, but facilitating degree completion is not one of them.

Progress and "Swirl"

There is a strong temporal element in Adelman's (1999, 2006) work. This is clear from his longitudinal perspective and his interest in academic history, in the importance he attaches to continuous enrollment (not just within institutions or sectors but between them), in the differential completion patterns of full-time and part-time students, and in the importance of the academic calendar.

Adelman (1999, 2006) has also drawn attention to the growing complexity of postsecondary attendance patterns and, following Borden (2004), the larger phenomenon of student "swirl." It is a tendency that will continue to be reinforced by economic and demographic factors as larger numbers of students are pushed into part-time attendance status and combining their studies with employment. The likelihood is that this will contribute further to the fragmentation of postsecondary student experiences and outcomes. It is a tension that Adelman does not fully reconcile. Still, in his distinction between purposeful transfer and multi-institution attendance, his appeals to have retention rates follow students rather than institutions, and his focus on the "structures of opportunity," he has carved out a new framework for analysis and action. It is one that directs attention to academic structures and arrangements rather than culture, to demonstrable performance and behavior rather than the more elusive notion of student experience, and to the levers at an institution's disposal to affect outcomes. This is not an either/or, of course. Adelman fully recognizes the importance of culture and the complexity of background characteristics that shape student retention. Very simply, they were beyond the scope of his national longitudinal studies. They also tend to be beyond the control of college administrators and to that extent are unlikely to generate real institutional traction.

Conceptually, at least, there is a direct line from Adelman to the agenda for Complete College America as it works with states to address the college completion shortfall. Its most recent report, *Time is the Enemy* (Complete College America 2011), zeroes in on the temporal challenge. The challenge, following Adelman (1999, 2006), lies in greater numbers of part-time students, broken remediation programs, excess credits, and lengthening time to degree. The solutions echo Adelman, too: year-round scheduling, embedding remediation in the regular college curriculum, and online technology.

The solutions already adopted by a number of states include dual enrollment programming, overhauling placement and remediation programs and embedding remediation in college-level coursework, streamlining registration procedures (registering once in a course sequence rather than multiple times in disconnected courses), intensifying instruction, reducing exit points—particularly in remedial courses—and providing alternative pathways to the degree.

Some schools rely heavily on improved advising and the creation of clearer degree completion roadmaps, such as the University of Iowa's (n.d.) four-year degree plan, the University of Duluth's (2012) 30-60-90 program, or San Diego State University's move to encourage students to take a full-time load (Nguyen, Bibo, and Engle 2012). Others are making structural changes to provide greater alignment and continuity, as with the state of Florida's encouragement of dual enrollment and credit by examination using Advanced Placement and the International Baccalaureate (Florida Department of Education 2011), or the longstanding dual enrollment partnership between Oregon State University and Linn-Benton Community College (Bontrager, Clemetsen, and Watts 2005). Others still, such as the Tennessee Tech Centers, have increased completion in part by redesigning registration systems so that students now register for a complete academic program rather than on a course-by-course basis (Complete College America n.d.). Additionally, the California Acceleration Project (2012) is redesigning math and English courses to improve student progress to degree by mainstreaming students into college-level courses, providing alternatives to remediation, and compressing course sequences and reducing the number of likely exit points.

There are many reasons why students are taking longer to complete their degrees, but one of them is that they are required to earn more credits than was the case three or four decades ago (Johnson 2011). While some states and institutions have taken steps to control or even reduce unnecessary "credit creep," the fact remains that the four-year degree has long been a misnomer even for those who maintain full-time and continuous enrollment.

Creative uses of the academic calendar to reduce time to degree have been on the agenda for some years now, particularly in large public university systems. They have gained additional traction in recent years as public institutions have sought to minimize tuition increases in the wake of reduced state appropriations. For example, Purdue University has announced plans to move to a "balanced trimester" calendar (Purdue University 2012). This calendar converts the summer into a full term, allowing some students to complete their degrees in three years and others to continue with a four-year degree that would allow room for educationally purposeful experiences, such as internships and study abroad. The expectation at Purdue is that the more intentional use of the summer term to accelerate degree completion will also lead to substantial increases in revenue. As with course redesign, the institutional incentive is grounded in financial, as much as educational, considerations. There is a built-in tension here, and time will tell whether the pressure to increase revenue will undermine improved educational outcomes. But there is clearly potential to realize both.

The "Quality" of Persistence

Reframing college completion efforts around notions of progress rather than persistence does not imply a dismantling of traditional approaches to retention. Yet for many institutions it will require a change of focus. Much of what has been done in the name of improving student retention makes good educational sense and may also be justified on grounds of institutional mission and effectiveness. But graduating students—not merely retaining them—demands a new level of clarity and single-mindedness in terms of institutional thinking and effort. It will necessarily bring into sharper and systemic focus the student attendance patterns, academic performance, and enrollment trajectories (and bottlenecks) that most directly shape successful and timely degree completion.

Such a refocusing on core academic mechanisms that are clearly amenable to institutional control are at once consistent with Tinto's (1987) call to move retention efforts from the periphery to the center of campus attention and with an accountability agenda that is pushing postsecondary institutions to do a better job of educating and graduating the students they enroll. Indeed, it is a shift in perspective that is amply illustrated by his choice of book titles. His first (now classic) 1987 book was *Leaving College: Rethinking the Causes and Cures of Student Attrition*; his latest, published in 2012, is *Completing College: Rethinking Institutional Action*. Here Tinto fully acknowledges that greater attention needs to be paid to the "quality" of persistence.

> Our ability to help students stay in college and graduate depends not just on our being able to help them continue to the second year, but to do so with the credits, knowledge, and skills required for success beyond the first year. (2012, 147–48)

It is precisely this "quality" of persistence that a progress-based perspective brings into focus. It marks a shift of emphasis away from a conceptual model grounded in *culture* (e.g., transition, integration, experience, and engagement) to one that pays greater attention to the *structural* elements (e.g., administrative policies, academic calendars, course design, and curriculum pathways) that provide the essential conditions and framework for student achievement and completion. The point is not that institutional structure is more important than culture; it is hardly that. But in focusing so much on student integration and departure, traditional approaches to retention have relied on a definition of the situation that pays insufficient attention to core academic arrangements and practices, the information and data on how students navigate them, and the mechanisms for influencing them that are most amenable to institutional control. In highly idealized and dichotomous form, the contrast between the two perspectives may be illustrated as shown in Table 3.1.

Again, in drawing this contrast between two perspectives, the aim is not for one to supplant the other. Just as a narrow definition of persistence overvalues continued enrollment at the expense of academic achievement, a similarly narrow definition of progress might overvalue degree completion at the expense of a wider (or deeper) educational experience for some or serve as a constraint rather than a guide for others. When the costs of

Table 3.1. Contrasting Perspectives: Persistence Versus Progress

	Persistence-centered	Progress-centered
Perspective	Retention/attrition	Advancement to completion
Focus	Culture	Structure
Activity	Student services/intervention	Academic/administrative policies
Metrics	Descriptive	Analytical

non-completion both in terms of indebtedness and lost opportunity are so high, institutions have an obligation to provide clear and achievable pathways to degree attainment. Equally, there is nothing in a progress-based perspective that would diminish the need for programming to support student engagement and integration into the campus community. Improving student engagement is an important educational task and is likely to have positive retention outcomes. However, it remains a somewhat elusive concept with multiple definitions. Without focus and discipline it could provide cover for a great many institutional efforts with marginal aggregate effect.

With competing demands and limited resources, institutions need to be clear about what works in fostering timely progress to degree. One of the best ways to do that is to collect the sorts of data that invite questions and underwrite decision-making and strategy. While there is no shortage of retention research, much of it is descriptive, programmatic, or focused on variables that have minimal impact on degree completion. One of the obvious lessons of Adelman's (1999, 2006) work is that institutions should be collecting and analyzing data that have not always been associated with degree attainment, such as attendance and credit accumulation patterns, curricular gateways, summer enrollment, grade trends, and course withdrawals and repeats. Equally, institutions need to adopt a more analytical and perhaps contrarian attitude to their data. As we have discovered at DePaul, persistence is a very imperfect predictor of degree attainment. What really counts is academic performance in the first year, and even then only when grades are linked to credit accumulation. This is not something that could have been directly discerned from existing institutional reports without a process of questioning and of aligning data in new ways so as to illuminate deep-seated patterns and dynamics (Kalsbeek and Associates 2009).

A New Mental Model?

One of the underlying assumptions of this book is that the dominant mental models governing retention thinking, research, and practice need revision. As Peter Senge put it some years ago in his seminal book, *The Fifth Discipline* (1990, 8), mental models are the "deeply ingrained assumptions, generalizations, or even pictures or images, that influence how we understand the world and how we take action." The second part of that sentence is as important as the first: Mental models shape both the way we think and what we do. They may either enlarge or constrain our scope for understanding and action.

The basic point of this chapter is that our mental model of student retention has been at least partly shaped by our language. The term persistence has directed our attention to certain aspects of the retention puzzle, and in doing so it has pulled our attention away from others. Over time, the word has become so ubiquitous that we are no longer aware of its meanings or implications. Yet this is precisely how mental models work. As Adelman (2006, 106) reminds us, "language does more than reflect reality; it creates reality as well."

Nevertheless, we need mental models. The problems begin, as Senge (1990) argues, when they become unconscious or unexamined. This could be the case with progress just as much as it is with persistence, especially if it is defined in narrow accountability terms. The challenge, as Senge sees it, is to connect our mental models with other disciplines such as institutional learning and systems thinking. The discipline of working with mental models, he argues, starts with "turning the mirror inward," holding our assumptions and thinking up to scrutiny, and using that process as a way to stimulate collective inquiry and action. That is essentially what a 4 Ps framework of student retention is intended to do.

References

Adelman, C. 1999. *Answers in the Toolbox: Academic Intensity, Attendance Patterns, and Bachelor's Degree Attainment*. Washington, D.C.: U.S. Department of Education.

Adelman, C. 2006. *The Toolbox Revisited: Paths to Degree Completion from High School through College*. Washington, D.C.: U.S. Department of Education.

Alexander, K. L., M. A. Cook, and E. L. McDill. 1978. "Curriculum Tracking and Educational Stratification." *American Sociological Review* 43:47–66.

Astin, A. W. 1975. *Preventing Students from Dropping Out*. San Francisco: Jossey-Bass.

Astin, A. W. 1985. *Achieving Educational Excellence*. San Francisco: Jossey-Bass.

Bean, J. P. 1980. "Dropouts and Turnovers: The Synthesis and Test of a Causal Model of Student Attrition." *Research in Higher Education* 12(2):155–87.

Bontrager, B., B. Clemetsen, and T. Watts. 2005. "Enabling Student Swirl: A Community College/University Dual Enrollment Program." *College and University Journal* 80(4):3–6.

Borden, V. M. H. 2004. "Accommodating Student Swirl: When Traditional Students Are No Longer the Tradition." *Change* 36(2):10–16.

California Acceleration Project. 2012. "Why Acceleration?" Accessed August 29, 2012, http://cap.3csn.org/why-acceleration/.

Clinedinst, M. E., S. F. Hurley, and D. A. Hawkins. 2011. *2011 State of College Admission*. Washington, D.C.: National Association for College Admission Counseling.

Coca, V., D. Johnson, T. Kelley-Kemple, M. Roderick, E. Moeller, N. Williams, and K. Moragne. 2012. "Working to My Potential: The Post-Secondary Experiences of CPS Students in the International Baccalaureate Diploma Programme." Chicago: The University of Chicago Consortium on Chicago School Research.

Complete College America. 2011. "Time is the Enemy." Accessed August 29, 2012, http://www.completecollege.org/docs/Time_Is_the_Enemy.pdf.

Complete College America. n.d. "A Working Model for Student Success: The Tennessee Technology Centers." Accessed September 22, 2012, http://www.completecollege.org /docs/Tennessee%20Technology%20Centers-%20A%20Preliminary%20Case %20Study%281%29.pdf.

Durkheim, E. 1951. *Suicide: A Study In Sociology.* New York: The Free Press.

Florida Department of Education. 2011. "Statewide Articulation Manual." Accessed September 22, 2012, http://www.fldoe.org/articulation/pdf/statewide-postsecondary -articulation-manual.pdf.

Habley, W. R., J. L. Bloom, and S. Robbins. 2012. *Increasing Persistence.* San Francisco: Jossey-Bass.

Johnson, N. 2011. "Three Policies to Reduce Time to Degree." Complete College America. Accessed August 29, 2012, http://www.completecollege.org/docs/Three%20 Policies%20to%20Reduce%20Time%20to%20Degree%20-%20Nate%20Johnson.pdf.

Kalsbeek, D. H., and Associates. 2009, May. "Undergraduate Retention and Degree Completion: Exploring the Relationship of Academic Preparation, Performance and Progress, with Financial Need and Financial Aid on Retention and Degree Completion." Paper presented to the DePaul University Board of Trustees, Chicago.

Nguyen, M., E. W. Bibo, and J. Engle. 2012. *Advancing to Completion: Increasing Degree Attainment by Improving Graduation Rates and Closing Gaps for Hispanic Students.* Washington, D.C.: The Education Trust.

Purdue University. 2012. "Purdue Trimester Plan Will Accelerate Time-To-Degree, Enhance Educational Opportunities." Accessed September 22, 2012, http://www .purdue.edu/newsroom/academics/2012/120111CordovaTrimester.html.

Senge, P. M. 1990. *The Fifth Discipline: The Art and Practice of the Learning Organization.* New York: Currency Doubleday.

Spady, W. 1970. "Dropouts from Higher Education: An Interdisciplinary Review and Synthesis." *Interchange* 1(1):64–85.

Tierney, W. G. 1999. "Models of Minority College-Going and Retention: Cultural Integrity versus Cultural Suicide." *Journal of Negro Education* 68(1):80–91.

Tinto, V. 1987. *Leaving College: Rethinking the Causes and Cures of Student Attrition.* Chicago: The University of Chicago Press.

Tinto, V. 2005, July. "Student Retention: What Next?" Paper presented at the National Conference on Student Recruitment, Marketing and Retention, Washington, D.C.

Tinto, V. 2012. *Completing College: Rethinking Institutional Action.* Chicago: The University of Chicago Press.

Twigg, C. 2005. *Increasing Success for Underserved Students: Redesigning Introductory Courses.* Saratoga Springs, N.Y.: National Center for Academic Transformation.

University of Duluth. 2012. "30-60-90 Student Success Roadmap." Accessed August 29, 2012, http://www.d.umn.edu/roadmap/.

University of Iowa. n.d. "Four Year Graduation Plan." Accessed August 29, 2012, http:// www.uiowa.edu/web/advisingcenter/fouryeargraduationplan.htm.

Van Gennep, A. 1960. *The Rites of Passage.* Chicago: The University of Chicago Press.

BRIAN SPITTLE *is the assistant vice president for the Center for Access and Attainment within the division of Enrollment Management and Marketing at DePaul University.*

4

The third "P" within a 4 Ps framework of student retention—process—gives priority attention to institutional processes and policies that either help or hinder the continuous enrollment of all students, not just students defined as "at risk."

Reframing Retention Strategy: A Focus on Process

Charles C. Schroeder

Introduction

When institutions engage in discussions regarding improving retention and graduation rates, invariably the conversation focuses on entering student characteristics, especially ACT and SAT scores and high school grades. Who among us has not heard this familiar refrain: "If we only had better students, we'd be a much better institution!" Clearly, attracting and enrolling well-prepared and motivated high-ability students will certainly improve institutional measures of academic achievement and time to degree. However, if one accepts the premise that degree completion is also an outcome of a high-quality undergraduate experience broadly defined, then institutions must focus attention on students' encounters with broad processes more than simply inputs. Indeed, if graduation is the primary metric by which institutional performance should be judged, then one has to ponder this question: "What kinds of empowering institutional processes produce the most desirable results for the majority of students?"

This chapter underscores the importance of creating broad-based, empowering undergraduate experiences that intentionally foster a higher level of success for large numbers of students—the *process* component of a 4 Ps framework. By focusing more on processes than isolated, discrete activities, institutions can create shared responsibility for educational quality and productivity.

New Directions for Higher Education, no. 161, Spring 2013 © Wiley Periodicals, Inc.
Published online in Wiley Online Library (wileyonlinelibrary.com) • DOI:10.1002/he.20044

Key Organizational Challenges, Principles, and Conceptual Frameworks

A primary assumption of this book is that improving broad processes affecting the largest number of students is the optimal institutional focus for increasing rates of retention and degree completion. The obstacles are a variety of common organizational realities including: (a) highly fragmented, compartmentalized, and insular structures that restrict communication, coordination, and collective responsibility; (b) deeply rooted cultural differences about what matters most in undergraduate education between and among faculties and their student- and administrative-affairs counterparts; (c) absence of timely, relevant data to inform and guide institutional policy discussions and strategic improvement efforts; (d) lack of clear vision and unwavering senior leadership regarding the centrality of educational attainment as an institutional imperative; (e) limited cross-functional alignments and traditional tendencies to focus more on discrete activities than preferred outcomes; and (f) the "tyranny of custom"—that is, the comfort and predictability derived from doing things the same way regardless of whether they are producing desirable results (Groccia and Miller 2005; Schroeder, Nicholls, and Kuh 1983). In view of these institutional obstacles to facilitating higher graduation rates, what principles could help foster process-oriented, broad-based support for making substantial improvements in those rates?

In his book *Once Upon a Campus: Lessons for Improving Quality and Productivity in Higher Education*, Daniel Seymour (2002) delineates 14 "lessons" for framing institutional strategies for improving productivity. Although all are germane to the primary premise of this chapter, the following five are of particular significance:

1. *Begin with the end in mind.* A criticism often leveled at colleges and universities is that they are goal free and data averse. If improving graduation rates is an institutional aspiration, then is this aim valued, transparent, and consistently communicated to all institutional stakeholders who should contribute to its attainment? Do academic deans, for example, know the retention and graduation rates of their majors? Are they expected to develop college-based strategic improvement processes that are linked and aligned with the institution's graduation goals? Without clear aims, there is no shared understanding of what is truly important and hence little chance of making major institutional improvements.

2. *Left to our own devices, we pay too much attention to things of too little importance to the customer.* Students encounter a multitude of policies, practices, programs, and processes that influence their educational attainment. Institutions that understand their impact from student users' perspectives have the best chance to improve their efficacy. This

requires shifting an institution's orientation from one that is faculty- and staff-centered to one that embodies value-added, student-centered perspectives on organizational processes. Similarly, using systematic assessment to understand students' transactions and the learning, satisfaction, and success derived from them is a critical component of the shift as well.

3. *Waste is the unintended consequence of unattended work processes.* This lesson has three components. First, waste is that which adds cost without adding value. Second, a process is simply a method for doing things. Finally, "unattended" means that the process has no owner and/ or is not being monitored. How much waste, for example, occurs as a result of the impact of poor curriculum planning, ineffective advising, and inadequate course offerings on students' ability to fulfill degree requirements in a timely fashion? By adopting a process orientation, institutions can focus on learning and improving by taking a horizontal view of effectiveness rather than the customary, functional, and vertical one displayed in campus organizational charts.

4. *An organization is a relay team; the better the handoffs, the better the results.* A relay race is a process involving multiple runners with one compelling aim—winning the race. Winning, however, is not predicated solely on speed, but rather on how effectively the baton is passed between runners. In our highly specialized, fragmented, and decentralized organizations, runners (units) usually go in different directions (multiple and divergent aims) often with limited knowledge of the baton or the necessity of smooth handoffs. How effective, for example, are the handoffs between the first and second year; freshman advising and advising in the major; curriculum planning and course availability; admission, financial aid, advising, registration, and student accounts? While differentiation of roles and responsibilities is an organizational necessity, without a unified awareness of and commitment to enhancing process management, little progress will be made in improving time to degree.

5. *To create the future, change the past.* A 4 Ps framework attempts to reframe retention by challenging prevailing assumptions and focusing greater attention on institutional improvement. A maxim from the field of organizational learning suggests that "most organizations have shared assumptions (i.e., mental models) that protect the status quo and provide few opportunities for learning. Standard operating procedures can become so institutionalized that competence becomes associated with how well one adheres to the rules" (Seymour 2002, 101). This lesson suggests that enhancing degree completion rates is not a function of business as usual, but rather requires engaging in new business, such as out-of-the-box, systemic thinking. Not surprisingly, this requires a renewal process in which cross-functional dialogue is used to bring to the surface deeply held assumptions about what matters in the student experience.

The following section presents some well-established theoretical and conceptual frameworks for overcoming these challenges and for applying Seymour's (2002) lessons to create empowering encounters that enhance students' educational attainment and degree completion. Indeed, these models and frameworks can guide the development of comprehensive approaches to the question raised in the first paragraph of this chapter: "What kinds of empowering institutional processes produce the most desirable results for the majority of students?"

Conceptual Underpinnings

Over 75 years ago, Kurt Lewin (1936) introduced his "interactionist" framework, which is represented by the formula $B=f(P \times E)$, where behavior (B) is a function (f) of the interaction (x) between persons (P) and an environment (E). Lewin's approach conceptualizes human behavior as an outcome of the interactions between individual characteristics and environmental conditions. For example, if lower ability students are assigned advanced calculus classes, they are overwhelmed by course complexity and rigor. Conversely, if higher ability students are assigned remedial math courses, they are bored due to lack of intellectual stimulation. Creating calibrated schedules that account for differences in entering abilities and the differential demands of the courses will substantially increase the probability of success for all. Lewin's framework served as a foundation for the campus ecology perspective (Banning 1978; Strange and Banning 2001), which emphasizes the critical role that student-environment congruence or "fit" plays in fostering or inhibiting student success. The ecological perspective challenges institutional assumptions that students are the primary problem limiting educational attainment rather than incongruent, ineffective institutional conditions and processes. This is akin to asserting that if the shoe doesn't fit, there must be something wrong with the foot! Acknowledging the significance of environmental impacts, Astin's (1993) research on student involvement is based on his input-environment-outcome (I-E-O) model. Finally, Tinto's (1993) theory of institutional departure shares features of these frameworks and like them stresses the critical nature of environmental influences on student success.

Implications of these frameworks for higher education practice have been championed in compelling ways by numerous reformers, but none more eloquently than Russell Edgerton, long-time president of the American Association of Higher Education (AAHE). Edgerton (1986, 11) challenged us to examine our fundamental purpose—the "why" of undergraduate education by advancing the following three propositions:

> First, our mission is to design an undergraduate experience that is truly empowering; second, we must measure our success as educators on the basis of the quality of encounters we arrange inside and outside the classroom;

NEW DIRECTIONS FOR HIGHER EDUCATION • DOI:10.1002/he

and, third, if quality lies in the encounters we arrange, then we must ensure
that these encounters are powerful, even transformational ones.

These propositions challenge many fundamental assumptions and
mental models that traditionally drive institutional efforts. Historically,
institutions have placed most of their attention on individual students
while neglecting the importance of campus conditions in promoting their
learning and educational attainment. While inputs and outcomes are
important, Edgerton (1986) calls upon institutions to focus primary attention on the quality of student encounters, the interactions between the two,
or the "x" in Lewin's (1936) framework and the "E" in Astin's (1993). To be
sure, Edgerton impels institutions to focus on the quality of the student
experience broadly defined to include in- and out-of-class experiences and
the potential synergy that can be created between the two. This is a particularly important assertion because most institutions have little control over
the academic and other characteristics of the entering student cohort. They
can, however, significantly influence the nature and quality of students'
educational encounters from entry to exit in a variety of settings. Even
more so, institutions have the ability to influence and administer quality
institutional processes and policies that affect students' experiences as they
move through the institution.

The following section describes one high-impact institutional initiative
that substantially improved retention and graduation rates, highlighting the
value of a comprehensive, collaborative, and integrated campus commitment to improving graduation rates through a focus on broad, multidimen-
sional processes and student-institutional encounters.

Creating Seamless Learning Environments
for First-Year Students

In 1992, the University of Missouri–Columbia (MU), a Research I university, hired a new chancellor who immediately established a goal of "recap-
turing the public's trust" by reinvigorating undergraduate education. At the
same time, the University chose to become a "selective" institution and
thereby agreed to meet two performance standards established by the state's
Coordinating Board for Higher Education (CBHE): (1) a freshman-to-
sophomore retention rate of 85 percent, with all students completing 24
credit hours with a 2.0 GPA or better; and (2) a six-year graduation rate of
65 percent. MU's rates for retention and six-year graduation were 78 and
59 percent, respectively, in 1992.

At the same time, the size of the freshman class had declined precipi-
tously in preceding years resulting in residence hall occupancy falling from
6,200 to 4,100 residents, and three of nineteen residence halls had been
closed. Furthermore, the associate dean of the College of Arts and Sciences
was having difficulty predicting demand for required general education

courses, and some faculty and department chairs were concerned about declining levels of academic engagement, especially in the sciences. To address these challenges, senior leaders from student affairs, the college of arts and sciences, and the biology department formed a cross-functional, learning community planning team that designed and implemented a pilot freshman interest group (FIG) program that would accomplish the following objectives: (1) substantially enhance academic achievement, retention, and educational attainment (graduation) for freshmen; (2) make the large campus feel small by creating peer reference groups of students; (3) integrate curricular and cocurricular experiences through the development of seamless learning environments; (4) provide a means for admitted students to register early for their fall classes; and (5) encourage faculty to integrate ideas, content, writing, and research from various disciplines, thereby enhancing general education outcomes for students.

The learning communities, or FIGs, are small groups of students (usually 20), each of which take three core general education courses that address a particular theme, such as Women in Engineering, Science and Society, or Ancient People and Cultures. In addition, they take Interdisciplinary Studies 1: Freshman Pro-seminar. FIG students are assigned to the same residence hall community and co-enroll in the same sections of the three core courses. Each FIG has an undergraduate peer advisor who lives with the students and helps them with the transition to college; their peer advisor also co-teaches with a faculty member in one of the three core courses or the Pro-seminar.

The program was initiated with twelve FIGs enrolling approximately 250 students; however, due to the program's initial success it was rapidly expanded to include not only FIGs, but sponsored learning communities (e.g., World of Business) and residential colleges (e.g., Science and Mathematics) as well. During the past 15 years, about 70 percent of each entering class has participated in some form of a learning community with approximately 20,000 students having been affiliated with one or more communities. Currently, MU sponsors more than 150 diverse learning communities for entering and continuing residential students.

Have these learning communities improved retention and graduation rates? The answer is a resounding "yes." In a longitudinal study (Beckett 2006) that included all entering students (13,000+) from 1998–2001, while controlling for a range of entering characteristics, such as ethnicity, high school GPA, family income, etc., students in FIGs achieved significantly higher retention and graduation rates. For example, six-year graduation rates for FIG participants were 69 percent compared with 62 percent for students not in FIGs. Similar results were recorded regarding four-year rates with FIG participants achieving a 46 percent rate compared with a 39 percent rate for non-participants. For "at-risk" students in the sample— those with a family income of less than $48,000 or a high school GPA below 2.75—51 percent earned a degree, but the graduation rates of those students who participated in a FIG (59 percent) and those who were not in a FIG (48 percent) differed by about 11 percent. In addition, students of color achieved significantly higher grades as well as retention and graduation rates than their Caucasian counterparts. Empirical research conducted at different times during the past 15 years has also confirmed that FIG participants are much more engaged intellectually, achieve higher GPAs, demonstrate greater academic integration and institutional commitment, exhibit higher levels of interactions with peers and faculty, demonstrate much greater gains in general education outcomes, and are more satisfied with various aspects of their undergraduate experiences (Pike, Schroeder, and Berry 1997; Purdie 2007; Schroeder 2005; Schroeder, Minor, and Tarkow 1999). And, perhaps most importantly, this comprehensive and ongoing learning community initiative enabled MU to fulfill in a timely fashion its obligation to meeting the CBHE performance standards of an 85 percent retention rate and 65 percent six-year graduation rate.

During the past ten years, other large institutions, such as Indiana University, Auburn University, the University of Texas–Austin, and Saint Louis University among many others, have launched similar, large-scale, and comprehensive learning community programs in an effort to improve academic achievement, retention, and graduation rates. However, institutions of all sizes appear to benefit from this institutional strategy (Brower and Inkelas 2010; Knight 2003; Kuh 2008; Kuh et al. 2005; Pence, Workman, and Haruta 2005; Smith et al. 2004; Stassen 2003; Upcraft, Gardner, and Barefoot 2005). For example, a smaller, public institution, Christopher Newport University (CNU), implemented learning communities in 2005 and over the next two years increased the overall first- to second-year retention rate dramatically. Learning communities added 10 percent to retention and 8 percent to four-year graduation rates. The program was so successful that in 2010, CNU required all 1,200 entering students to participate in some form of learning community.

Learning communities are clearly one of the most low-cost yet high-impact strategies available to all kinds of institutions, from community colleges to comprehensive research universities that are interested in substantially improving student success. Their efficacy results from using pedagogies of active engagement to impel higher levels of interaction in educationally purposeful activities among students in non-traditional, out-of-class settings such as residence halls. Clearly, learning communities intentionally connect curricular and cocurricular experiences in a complementary, mutually supportive, and integrated fashion thereby illustrating the critical importance of linking and aligning powerful, purposeful encounters (x) between students (P) and environmental experiences (E) that influence their success.

Conclusion

In view of the major challenges currently affecting all segments of higher education such as calls for accountability, skyrocketing costs, shifting demographics, and changing economic agendas, it is time to shift our campus conversations from "doing more with less" to "doing less with less—but well." A campus orientation to the importance of process requires us to leave the comfort and predictability of bureaucratic and fragmented organizational structures and focus on the functional interconnectedness of students' interactions with all aspects of their experiences: academic, cocurricular, and administrative. To do so, we must create and shape environmental conditions and processes that direct, nurture, and sustain powerful and hopefully transformational encounters for all students. Successful institutional examples are offered in chapter 7, illustrating that such process-focused efforts are not only possible—they are also powerful in improving student retention and completion rates.

References

Astin, A. 1993. *What Matters in College? Four Critical Years Revisited*. San Francisco: Jossey-Bass.

Banning, J. H., ed. 1978. *Campus Ecology: A Perspective for Student Affairs*. Cincinnati: NASPA Monograph.

Beckett, A. 2006. "Relationship Between Participation in a Residentially-Based Freshman Interest Group and Degree Attainment." PhD diss., University of Missouri.

Brower, A. M., and K. K. Inkelas. 2010. "Living-Learning: One High Impact Educational Practice." *Liberal Education* 96(2):35–43.

Edgerton, R. 1986. "Closing Convictions." *AAHE Bulletin* 38(10):7–12.

Groccia, J. E., and J. E. Miller. 2005. *On Becoming a Productive University: Strategies for Reducing Costs and Increasing Quality in Higher Education*. Bolton, Mass.: Anker Publishing.

Knight, W. 2003. "Learning Communities and First-Year Programs: Lessons for Planners." *Planning for Higher Education* 31(4):5–12.

Kuh, G. D. 2008. *High-Impact Educational Practices: What They Are, Who Has Access to Them, and Why They Matter*. Washington, D.C.: Association of American Colleges and Universities.

Kuh, G. D., J. Kinzie, J. H. Schuh, E. J. Whitt, and Associates. 2005. *Student Success in College: Creating Conditions That Matter*. San Francisco: Jossey-Bass.

Lewin, K. 1936. *Principles of Typological Psychology*. New York: McGraw-Hill.

Pence, L., H. Workman, and M. Haruta. 2005. "A General Chemistry and Precalculus First-Year Interest Group (LC): Effect on Retention, Skills, and Attitudes." *Journal of Chemical Education* 82(1):65–69.

Pike, G. R., C. C. Schroeder, and T. R. Berry. 1997. "Enhancing the Educational Impact of Residence Halls: The Relationship Between Residential Learning Communities and First-Year College Experiences and Persistence." *Journal of College Student Development* 38:609–621.

Purdie, J. R. 2007. "Examining the Academic Performance and Retention of First-Year Students in Living Learning Communities, Freshmen Interest Groups, and First-Year Experience Courses." PhD diss., University of Missouri.

Schroeder, C. C. 2005. "Collaborative Partnerships Between Academic and Student Affairs." In *Challenging and Supporting the First-Year Student: A Handbook for Improving the First Year of College,* edited by M. L. Upcraft, J. N. Gardner, and B. O. Barefoot, 204–220. San Francisco: Jossey-Bass.

Schroeder, C. C., F. D. Minor, and T. A. Tarkow. 1999. "Learning Communities: Partnerships Between Academic and Student Affairs." In *Learning Communities: New*

Structures, New Partnerships for Learning, edited by J. H. Levine, 59–69. Columbia: University of South Carolina, National Resource Center for the First-Year Experience and Students in Transition.

Schroeder, C. C., G. E. Nicholls, and G. D. Kuh. 1983. "Exploring the Rainforest: Testing Assumptions and Taking Risks." In *Understanding Student Affairs Organizations*, New Directions for Student Services, no. 23, edited by G. D. Kuh, 51–61. San Francisco: Jossey-Bass.

Seymour, D. 2002. *Once Upon a Campus: Lessons for Improving Quality and Productivity in Higher Education*. Westport, Conn.: American Council on Education / The Oryx Press.

Smith, B. L., J. MacGregor, R. S. Matthews, and F. Gablenick. 2004. *Learning Communities: Reforming Undergraduate Education*. San Francisco: Jossey-Bass.

Stassen, M. L. 2003. "Student Outcomes: The Impact of Varying Living-Learning Community Models." *Research in Higher Education* 44(5):581–612.

Strange, C. C., and J. H. Banning. 2001. *Educating by Design: Creating Campus Learning Environments That Work*. San Francisco: Jossey-Bass.

Tinto, V. 1993. *Leaving College: Rethinking the Causes and Cures of Student Attrition*. Chicago: The University of Chicago Press.

Upcraft, M. L., J. N. Gardner, and B. O. Barefoot. 2005. *Challenging and Supporting the First-Year Student: A Handbook for Improving the First Year of College*. San Francisco: Jossey-Bass.

CHARLES C. SCHROEDER is a senior associate consultant for Noel-Levitz specializing in retention and student success strategies and interventions.

5

The fourth "P" within a 4 Ps framework of student retention—promise—connects retention strategies with institutional brand strategies so that marketing and retention become mutually reinforcing.

Reframing Retention Strategy: A Focus on Promise

David H. Kalsbeek

Introduction

At every college and university, students enroll with expectations and aspirations about the kind of experience and the kind of outcomes that the institution delivers. When those expectations are met and exceeded, students are satisfied and likely to remain committed to their college choice. When their experience falls short of their expectations, their commitment to the institution erodes and attrition can be the outcome of those unmet expectations.

Students' expectations for their college experience are shaped in many ways, including by what the marketing industry would call the institution's brand identity and brand promise—its distinctive value proposition as perceived by the students. The importance and influence of brand in consumer behavior is undeniable, and the role of institutional brand in students' initial and continuous enrollment choices is no different. Market research shows the impact that institutional brand has on students' initial college choice. Once enrolled, their initial enrollment choice is continuously solidified and enhanced by their positive experience of and satisfaction with the institution's brand promise.

Today, more than ever, it is essential for institutions to define and differentiate themselves in the marketplace, and they do so by demonstrably delivering on their distin ctive promise. A positive and brand-congruent experience not only benefits the student, it reinforces that institution's brand identity; conversely, a student experience that is incongruent with the brand promise not only leads to student dissatisfaction, it also erodes that brand.

NEW DIRECTIONS FOR HIGHER EDUCATION, no. 161, Spring 2013 © Wiley Periodicals, Inc.
Published online in Wiley Online Library (wileyonlinelibrary.com) • DOI:10.1002/he.20045

The process of brand development can help provide a retention effort with a strategic market orientation focused on overarching institutional outcomes rather than on narrowly individualized student outcomes, an orientation that can help the retention effort gain traction and connection with broader purposes. Within a 4 Ps framework, a research-based focus on the institutional brand promise can bring together retention and institutional marketing, and strategically linking the two completes and integrates the entire enrollment life cycle.

Setting the Stage

There are several conceptual underpinnings for focusing on *promise* in framing an institutional approach to retention.

First, in even the earliest conceptualizations and representations of retention theory, it is acknowledged that the fit between students (each with their particular expectations and aspirations) and institutions (each with their particular academic and social environments) is an important ingredient in understanding student departure. Tinto's models (1993) orient retention strategy toward the academic and social integration of students and institutions, focusing on ensuring some optimal congruence between expectations and experience as students and institutions interact. This parallels the work of person-environment interaction theories about student development (Schroeder 1981; Walsh 1973). All of this suggests that to the extent attrition is a function of unmet student expectations, a retention strategy must focus on how those expectations are set and ensure the congruence of student and institutional expectations and experiences. At the institutional level, retention strategy should ask: "What expectations do students bring regarding their likely experiences and outcomes at the institution?"; "Are those expectations congruent with the institution's purposes and priorities?"; and "Is the lived experience and interaction between the student and the institution consistent with what each values?" All of these questions, fundamentally, are the same questions asked when developing a brand marketing strategy.

Another perspective on *promise* is the connection of learning outcomes and retention. Colleges and universities, students and families, employers and communities, governments and societies all place value on the learning outcomes of higher education. Educational outcomes and the benefits they create are at the foundation of what institutions of higher education offer, are fundamentally what students seek, and are the desired outcomes of the various publics that fund and support higher education. Learning outcomes are, in fact, the core of the institution's educational promise. As an increasingly mature industry (Levine 2001), higher education faces growing pressure to ensure that it delivers demonstrable educational outcomes; the importance of defining and ensuring the promise of higher education was articulated by the Spellings Commission's report, *A Test of Leadership:*

Charting the Future of U.S. Higher Education (2006) and is explored by Caryn Chaden in chapter 9 of this volume.

Finally, the emergence of enrollment management (EM) as an approach to institutional improvement introduces another perspective on *promise* as it integrates marketing and retention. While the practice of EM has evolved considerably over the last 30 years, by definition it has consistently sought to focus on the entire life cycle of student enrollment—from the earliest stages of marketing, recruitment, and admission through retention to degree completion and even beyond (Hossler 1984; Kalsbeek and Hossler 2009). An EM perspective integrates everything from how the institution defines and develops its distinct identity and brand to how the student experience in and out of the classroom reflects that brand promise. Ensuring such integration and complementarity is the defining nature of EM in theory and in practice and supports the strategic value of linking retention and brand marketing.

From these several distinct strands, one can weave a context within which the brand promise and the art and science of brand marketing become integral in mobilizing retention strategy at the institutional level. Brand marketing perspectives, born in the consumer products industry, long ago crossed into institutional marketing strategy in higher education. They now create an effective avenue for ensuring that retention efforts not only improve student success and institutional enrollment outcomes, but also elevate the institutional brand and achieve its promise.

Brand as Promise

The concept of brand equity, introduced by David Aaker in the late 1980s, has revolutionized the way that consumer products companies measure success. Brand equity is defined by Aaker (1991) as the assets linked to a brand's name or symbol that adds to a product or service. Traditionally, sales were the ultimate, and only, measure of a company's collective efforts to meet a market need. Today, most organizations view their brands as strategic assets that create competitive advantage and build long-term profitability. The importance of brand equity now has a role that parallels sales when measuring a for-profit company's overall value.

Brand equity is found in the brand identity, which according to Aaker and Joachimsthaler (2009, 40), is "aspirational" and "represents what the organization wants the brand to stand for." The brand identity is a set of associations that imply a promise from the organization to its customers. To have value, a brand's identity must resonate with its customer base, help differentiate itself from the competition, and clarify what the organization can and will do over time. When a brand's promise is kept, the relationship between the brand and its customer deepens, resulting in loyalty, sales, and recommendations to future customers. If the brand delivers on its promise, the customer's expectation will have been met and a loyal customer will have been created. If not, the customer moves on.

NEW DIRECTIONS FOR HIGHER EDUCATION • DOI:10.1002/he

As the discipline of brand strategy has expanded to traditionally "non-marketing-oriented" industries such as higher education, so has the misconception that brands can be "created." But at its core, brand is more a noun than a verb (Ries and Ries 1998); it is something that exists in the eyes and minds of key constituencies, not something an organization simply chooses to say about itself. Identifying which brand associations to leverage and how to articulate the brand promise requires an assessment of an organization's brand through the eyes of its customers and through the eyes of other stakeholders and key audiences, as well as a comparison of current and potential competitors. By studying the brand from these multiple perspectives, an organization can clarify what it does well, how it meets the needs of its customers better than the competition, and if the potential customer is able to evaluate whether they are interested in engaging with the brand based on these brand associations and attributes.

Therefore, in Aaker and Joachimsthaler's (2009) approach to brand building, the first step is to understand how the institution is perceived currently and determine how it wants to be perceived in the future. In higher education, that requires studies with key constituent groups—prospective students, parents, current students, alumni, high school counselors, employers, and community leaders—to help clarify the positive associations to leverage and the negative associations to overcome. Determining the brand's functional and tangible benefits as well as emotional benefits provided to various groups defines the overall value proposition, or promise, that they expect in their interactions with the institution. One example in higher education is the brand strategy developed by American University (AU; 2012), resulting in its "American Wonk" brand marketing campaign. The comprehensive process underlying the development of its marketing campaign was grounded in an assessment of AU's distinctive culture and the lived experience of students, faculty, and alumni; and the market research process discovered and distilled AU's distinctive brand identity and framed its brand promise in a way that resonates with AU's multiple audiences.

Similar to the consumer products industry, the more perceptions and expectations of the college or university brand align with the benefits students seek, the greater the value students perceive in their education and the greater the likelihood of outcomes such as student retention, stronger alumni loyalty and support, and positive word-of-mouth recommendations. The brand can and should then be managed and leveraged as a strategic asset and directly tied to tangible student and institutional outcomes. While a strategic brand analysis and the development of the overall brand strategy can require significant investment, the efforts to deliver on that brand promise based on the analysis can become far more focused and therefore more cost-effective and efficient over time. Admission and marketing efforts can focus on what is most important to students and other key constituent groups. Student affairs professionals can assess student experiences in light of the brand promise. Faculty and academic advisors can also measure their efforts to ensure a distinctive educational experience in light of student perceptions and expectations. Periodic monitoring of student perceptions and experiences and annual brand metrics sustains the value of brand equity in institutional strategy; these metrics include awareness of the institution, perception of key brand tenets and associations, satisfaction with those brand tenets, as well as propensity to recommend the brand. A brand strategy thereby contributes to a sustainable business practice.

Linking Brand Promise and Retention

Institutional retention strategies typically acknowledge the importance of ensuring students' satisfaction with their experience at the institution on the premise that student dissatisfaction leads to attrition. Therefore, student satisfaction surveys are common measures used in campus retention efforts (Schreiner 2009). Not surprisingly, such surveys tend to show higher satisfaction with the institution among "persisters" than among those who drop out. Retention leaders also often use survey research such as the College Student Experiences Questionnaire (CSEQ; 2007) or the National Survey of Student Engagement (NSSE; 2012) to assess the nature of the student experience itself, such as the frequency of student participation in various activities and the level of student engagement in academic and cocurricular life. Statistical analyses from such survey data seek to determine which activities correlate with greater likelihood of persistence and where there are opportunities to improve student satisfaction.

When retention strategy starts with the brand promise, however, it takes a step back and first asks: "What are the experiences and the outcomes that are most closely associated with our institutional brand?"; "To what degree do our students have the experiences and outcomes that our brand promise leads them to expect?"; and "How can we more intentionally ensure that the student's lived experience is congruent with that brand promise?"

From a brand promise perspective, the pursuit of student satisfaction in general terms is not sufficient for connecting retention efforts with broader institutional purposes. However, ensuring that students have satisfactory experiences in the areas that are most clearly aligned with the institutional brand is important; this is a step toward linking and leveraging retention strategies for broader institutional improvement beyond retention rates, since experiences that satisfactorily deliver the brand's promise reinforce that promise and build a sustainable brand identity in the marketplace. In this sense, retention is not about satisfaction and student success abstractly defined; it is about fulfilling the institution's promise for particular kinds of student experiences and outcomes, a promise grounded in the distinct and differentiating dimensions of the institutional brand. This shifts the intended outcome from improving student satisfaction to strengthening institutional positioning.

One natural challenge at every campus is that there are competing interests between various constituent groups regarding what dimensions of the student experience are most important. Advocates for service learning, for internationalization, for wellness, for student leadership, for multicultural programs, and for undergraduate research all vie for prominence in the student experience. Different groups advocate for requiring certain activities, for increasing funding for certain activities, or for giving academic credit for certain activities or preferential registration for students engaged in certain activities. All typically argue that a presumed positive impact on retention justifies that investment and priority and preferential attention, though actual evidence of any retention effect is often unavailable. Brokering the demands of these competing constituent groups is never easy, and it renders many retention strategies ill defined, diffused, and scattered.

However, bringing a brand marketing perspective to a retention strategy can provide necessary focus. In particular, brand research can offer a powerful litmus test for how various dimensions of the student experience resonate with the market realities of the institution's market position and for gauging which aspects of campus life have primacy in defining the institution's core identity, brand promise, and value proposition. Not all aspects of the student experience are created equal in terms of their consonance with the brand.

For example, years of market research at DePaul University have demonstrated empirically that three core tenets define the value proposition that year after year brings undergraduate students to DePaul: DePaul's rich urban immersion in Chicago, its practical education with extensive experiential learning and engagement opportunities, and its especially diverse student population. These three dimensions of the student experience shape why students choose DePaul over other institutions and are what they say make DePaul distinct and valuable. Urban, practical, and diverse are three elements, or tenets, at the heart of DePaul's brand promise.

Therefore, ensuring student satisfaction with these specific elements of the student experience takes precedence over others from a brand development perspective, since students' positive experiences in these domains not only benefit them individually, but also reinforce the distinct brand identity and brand promise that underlies DePaul's success in market differentiation. And when students discuss their positive college experiences through word of mouth, social media, and personal networks, that not only creates a positive impression of DePaul—it builds the brand.

On the other hand, student dissatisfaction with these particular experiences may lead to greater risk of attrition, since their experience falls short of their expectations and aspirations, and it risks eroding the University's brand promise and distinctiveness. Because market research shows these are the key differentiating elements of DePaul's identity and value proposition as it establishes its place in a cluttered marketplace of comprehensive universities in the region, dissatisfaction with those elements undercuts the brand. Efforts focused on these specific dimensions of the student experience therefore seek not only to improve student satisfaction, but also to reinforce a brand promise and thereby connect retention and marketing strategies at the institutional level.

One premise of a 4 Ps perspective is that if improving overall institution-wide outcomes is the intended goal, retention strategies should focus on the experiences of the many rather than the few, on the core of institutional purposes rather than on the margins. In chapter 8, George Kuh highlights several institutional examples in which colleges and universities have developed intentional approaches to ensuring that every student's experience reflects the distinct and differentiating nature of the institution's educational philosophy and purpose (i.e., the promise of the institutional brand). For example, Kuh's chapter offers Elon University as an illustration of an intentional integration of the student experience, student enrollment outcomes, institutional brand identity, and market differentiation.

Finding Promise in Mission

While intentionally linking retention efforts to brand marketing goals is an avenue for gaining traction in institutional retention strategy, the concept of "brand" may be more or less relevant to a college or university depending on that institution's profile and place in the market. As discussed in chapter 2, a 4 Ps perspective on student retention starts with an understanding of institutional market position. Returning to the work of Zemsky, Wegner, and Massy (2005), it can be argued that "brand value" is typically associated with institutions that, in fact, occupy a position with high market demand; in other words, having a brand identity is by definition a reflection of the institution's position in a stratified market. If Zemsky, Wegner, and Massy's so-called "medallion" institutions tend to have strong brands by definition (e.g., highly selective private research universities), middle-market institutions fight to develop and clarify their brand identities in order to stand out in a marketplace of undifferentiated competitors (Kalsbeek and Hossler 2009). In their aspiration to elevate their market position, middle-market schools engage in brand-building activities although the financial realities of their market position require them to remain responsive to conveniently available student demand.

The institutions in Zemsky, Wegner, and Massy's (2005) model that are in the open access, convenience, and locally based market segments (e.g., non-selective regional public universities) are the least likely to have a strong and differentiating brand identity. However, that doesn't mean that they lack a value proposition upon which a promise-oriented retention strategy can be built. Value propositions and promises can and often are also found in institutional mission. For many colleges and universities, the promise they seek to deliver for students is reflected not so much in a brand identity grounded in a market perspective but in a mission, a public charter, or an underlying institutional ethos or purpose.

In Kuh et al.'s (2005) work on student success, the authors refer specifically to the mission relevance of institutional purposes and how the mission can give "direction to all aspects of institutional life, including the policies and practices that foster student success" (25). Mission-oriented priorities are often difficult to discern in colleges and universities since they tend to be fairly broad statements of existential purpose and *raison d'être*. Advocates for any number of possible institutional foci can find support in most mission statements, despite the fact that those different foci may be inherently in conflict with each other. For example, mission-based rhetoric can push institutions simultaneously toward geographically broadening their national recruitment and also toward making the needs of the local community their highest priority; mission statements seldom can broker the inherent tensions between institutional aspirations for attracting the best students and for providing access and opportunity for the disadvantaged. Kuh et al. (2005, 26) argue that at the heart of those institutions that are effective in fostering student success is a pervasive commitment to an "enacted mission" reflected in the lived experience rather than the "espoused mission" reflected in mission statements, and the authors present multiple institutional examples of how a shared purpose shapes the distinct reality of the student experience.

This is again where the filter of brand research can enter the equation, even for institutions without a particularly notable brand identity. Brand research methods and techniques, such as those developed by Aaker and Joachimsthaler (2009), can help an institution view itself as various external audiences see it; such methods help put the institutional self-concept to the test of market research by gauging if its espoused values and purposes are in fact part of the institution's market identity in the eyes and minds of key constituencies. Using brand research to test if mission rhetoric matches the lived experience as well as the perceived institutional value creates a process by which a college or university becomes a more self-regarding institution (Ewell 1984). As both brand identity and mission priorities become clearer, so does the institutional promise—enabling retention strategy to become grounded in the core of institutional purpose.

Conclusion

A 4 Ps framework is intended to move retention strategy from the periphery to the center of institutional efforts by connecting retention with broader institutional dynamics. Directing retention strategy toward ensuring that the student experience is congruent with the institution's brand (and mission) helps move retention from being a sideshow into the center circle of how the institution defines itself and its purposes. Retention then becomes part of how the institution solidifies its distinct market position by amplifying its brand promise through the lived experience of its students.

References

Aaker, D. A. 1991. *Managing Brand Equity.* New York: The Free Press.

Aaker, D. A., and E. Joachimsthaler. 2009. *Brand Leadership: Building Assets in an Information Economy.* New York: The Free Press.

American University. 2012. "American Wonks." Accessed August 30, 2012, http://american wonks.com/why-wonk.

College Student Experiences Questionnaire. 2007. "CSEQ: General Info." Accessed August 30, 2012, http://cseq.iub.edu/cseq_generalinfo.cfm.

Ewell, P. 1984. *The Self-Regarding Institution: Information for Excellence.* Boulder, Colo: The National Center for Higher Education Management Systems.

Hossler, D. 1984. *Enrollment Management: An Integrated Approach.* New York: College Entrance Examination Board.

Kalsbeek, D. H., and D. Hossler. 2009. "Enrollment Management: A Market-Centered Perspective." *College and University Journal* 84(3):3–11.

Kuh, G. D., J. Kinzie, J. H. Schuh, E. J. Whitt, and Associates. 2005. *Student Success in College: Creating Conditions That Matter.* San Francisco: Jossey-Bass.

Levine, A. 2001. "Higher Education as a Mature Industry." In *In Defense of American Higher Education,* edited by P. G. Altbach, P. J. Gumport, and D. B. Johnstone, 38–58. Baltimore: The Johns Hopkins University Press.

National Survey of Student Engagement. 2012. "About NSSE." Accessed August 30, 2012, http://nsse.iub.edu/html/about.cfm.

Ries, L., and A. Ries. 1998. *The 22 Immutable Laws of Branding.* New York: HarperCollins.

Schreiner, L. A. 2009. *Linking Student Satisfaction and Retention.* Iowa City: Noel-Levitz.

Schroeder, C. C. 1981. "Student Development through Environmental Management." In *Increasing the Educational Role of Residence Halls,* New Directions for Student Services, no. 13, edited by G. Blimling and J. Schuh, 35–49. San Francisco: Jossey-Bass.

Spellings, M. 2006. *A Test of Leadership: Charting the Future of U.S. Higher Education.* Washington D.C.: U.S. Department of Education.

Tinto, V. 1993. *Leaving College: Rethinking the Causes and Cures of Student Attrition,* 2nd ed. Chicago: The University of Chicago Press.

Walsh, W. B. 1973. *Theories of Person-Environment Interaction: Implications for the College Student.* Iowa City: The American College Testing Program.

Zemsky, R., G. R. Wegner, and W. F. Massy. 2005. *Remaking the American University: Market-Smart and Mission-Centered.* Piscataway, N.J.: Rutgers University Press.

DAVID H. KALSBEEK is the senior vice president for the division of Enrollment Management and Marketing at DePaul University.

This chapter provides illustrations of a profile-oriented approach to retention through a discussion of test-optional policies and use of non-cognitive variables in the admission process.

Profile in Action: Linking Admission and Retention

Carla M. Cortes

A profile-oriented retention strategy embraces the admission process as a powerful lever in improving retention and completion rates and recognizes that the student profile can be shaped by changes in admission policies or priorities—even within the current market position of the institution. In addition, the student body can be oriented toward success and defined by retention and graduation through approaches that do not trade access for selectivity.

To undergird David Kalsbeek and Brian Zucker's chapter 2 on *profile* within a 4 Ps framework, one can return to an early exposition of the admission profession, thoughtfully presented by B. Alden Thresher, long-time dean of admissions at MIT. In a 1966 College Entrance Examination Board publication, *College Admission and the Public Interest*, Thresher presents a strong argument that predicting which students will be best qualified for a particular line of work, or even which students will in fact graduate, is less precise, less rational, and more fraught with difficulty than one might imagine; his premise holds true over forty years later. Thresher (1966, 1) lays out three assertions:

> First, one cannot tell by looking at a toad how far he will jump; second, the process of admission to college is more sociologically than intellectually determined; and third, to understand the process one must look beyond the purview of the individual college and consider the interaction of all institutions with the society that generates and sustains them.

Thresher's third point is similar to Kalsbeek and Zucker's discussion of the complex market landscape in which colleges find themselves, a context that somewhat limits colleges in their attempts to "admit graduates." It also

NEW DIRECTIONS FOR HIGHER EDUCATION, no. 161, Spring 2013 © Wiley Periodicals, Inc.
Published online in Wiley Online Library (wileyonlinelibrary.com) • DOI:10.1002/he.20046

recognizes the web of social institutions that interact to either constrain or propel students into various types of postsecondary opportunities. This chapter will suggest three approaches to a profile-oriented retention strategy, in relation to Thresher's prescient themes, through a discussion of test-optional policies, use of non-cognitive variables in the admission process, and varied approaches to curricular and degree pathways.

How Far Will the Toad Jump? Test-Optional Strategies

Admission, the process by which students sort into a range of postsecondary institutions based on mutual decisions about needs, scarcity, and reward, is often described as a combination of art and science. The science portion has perhaps been overly portrayed by the growing frenzy around college entrance tests, a perspective fueled by a testing industry grossing more than $4 billion annually (Soares 2012) and by the relentless push for prestige among colleges and universities (Lovett 2005; Schmidt 2008). Despite these forces, higher education institutions increasingly are recognizing that scores on standardized college admission exams, one of the presumed measures of students' academic readiness for college, fail to account for much variance in students' likelihood of graduating.

A growing body of research is challenging long-standing and tightly held assumptions about standardized tests. Numerous studies have concluded that while ACT or SAT scores are useful predictors of first-year college grades, standardized test scores alone are less predictive than the high school grade point average (HSGPA) (Adebayo 2008; Camara and Echternacht 2000; Kobrin et al. 2008; Zwick 2007). In *Crossing the Finish Line*, Bowen, Chingos, and McPherson (2009) affirm that HSGPA is the best predictor of graduation, *regardless of the quality of the high school*. In addition, high school grades are less closely correlated with students' socioeconomic characteristics than are standardized test scores (Bowen, Chingos, and McPherson 2009; Geiser and Santelices 2007).

Scholarly researchers have also known for quite some time that standardized test results have differential validity for various groups of students; this is not the same as "cultural bias" but indicates that the meaning of the results is not the same for all groups of students (Bowen and Bok 1998; Kobrin et al. 2008; Nankervis 2011; Zwick 2007). For example, ACT/SAT scores underpredict first-year grades for women and overpredict first-year grades for men (Camara and Echternacht 2000; Zwick 2007). The correlations of test scores with first-year grades tend to be somewhat smaller for black and Hispanic students than for white students (Zwick 2007). And it has been found that "much of the apparent predictive power of the SAT actually reflects the proxy effects of socioeconomic status" (Atkinson and Geiser 2012, 24), suggesting that the SAT may capture the stock of capital that wealthier students acquire throughout their lives.

NEW DIRECTIONS FOR HIGHER EDUCATION • DOI:10.1002/he

As a result, when test scores are used as "cut-points" for admission in general or honors and scholarship programs, small differences in scores can translate into meaningful differences in access for women, students of color, or low-income students. Test-oriented admission practices, therefore, only increase the obstacles to access without improving an institution's capacity to predict student success. As a result of these and other studies, the highly anticipated *Report of the Commission on the Use of Standardized Tests in Undergraduate Admission*, released in 2008 from the National Association for College Admission Counseling (NACAC), strongly recommended that colleges reconsider the use of standardized testing in their admission practices in the context of their own institutional missions and goals. This recommendation elevated the importance of including admission practices in an institution's retention strategy.

Numerous colleges heeded the NACAC advice in 2008 and completed their own validity studies; an increasing number began reducing their emphasis on test scores in college admission, with some adopting a test-optional approach. Joining a significant number of liberal arts colleges that were already test-optional, Wake Forest University, Sewanee–University of the South, Fairfield University, Loyola University–Maryland, New York University, and American University followed in quick succession, broadening the types of institutions implementing test-optional approaches. While test-optional institutions vary in what is required of students who choose not to submit test scores for admission, one facet is common to all: test-optional admission policies are designed to have a strong "signaling effect" to prospective students that a focus on learning throughout their entire high school career is the most valuable preparation for college completion and the best indicator of readiness for college.

Adopters of test-optional admission report that their applicants have become more diverse in racial, ethnic, and socioeconomic composition and in the range of expressed interests of study (Epstein 2009; Shanley 2007). Results from Bates College, Providence College, Mount Holyoke College, Worcester Polytechnic Institute, Pitzer College, Dickinson College, and Wake Forest University all show that students who did not submit test scores perform as well or better in terms of grades, retention, and degree attainment.

Recent data presented by two selective four-year institutions, Providence College and Dickinson College, reveal that a test-optional policy has been a win-win scenario for these institutions, especially in linking their admission goals with retention outcomes. At Providence College, 35 to 40 percent of enrolled students were admitted "test-optional," and the college enrolled more first-generation and Pell-eligible students as a result; students who did not submit test scores had slightly lower first-year retention than students who submitted scores (90.1 percent compared with 91.3 percent for student cohorts entering in 2011) but had slightly higher four-year graduation rates than students who submitted scores (83.7 percent compared with 82 percent; Lydon 2012). At Dickinson, data show that there is a difference in first-year college GPA between submitters and non-submitters (.3 higher for submitters). However, first-year retention is slightly higher for non-submitters (89 percent compared with 87 percent) despite the fact that the average composite ACT scores of students not submitting scores for the admission process were 5 to 6 points lower for the last several years (e.g., 24 for non-submitters versus 29 for submitters in 2011; Balmer 2012).

DePaul University, the largest private university to implement a test-optional program to date, conducted validity studies with an eye toward retention and degree completion, rather than just first-year grades. DePaul found that once HSGPA is known, ACT and SAT scores add little value in predicting "academic progress"—the critical combination of grades and credits earned in the first year (Cortes and Klaas 2011). Internal research at DePaul confirms that first-year "academic progress" is the key driver of retention and degree completion (Kalsbeek and Associates 2009).

Whether a student will persist, progress, and graduate is not highly predictable from any known pre-college factors; students are human beings who get homesick, have bad roommates, work too many hours at jobs, and have unexpected financial and personal stressors. A profile-centered retention strategy affirms that the best criterion that admissions officers have is the high school record, not test scores, to make an educated guess about how far the toad will jump.

Sociological Determinants and Non-Cognitive Variables

Common sense and observations of students in many educational contexts reveal that so-called "non-cognitive" student attributes are demonstrably important in accounting for student success. Students who stand out are those who work harder; are intrinsically motivated or curious; or persevere through challenges within the individual family setting or in the context of larger structural settings of poorly-resourced schools and communities kept to the margin by race, language, or economic barriers. A profile-oriented approach to admission and retention recognizes the strong and longitudinal impact of these sociological factors and seeks to understand how students both manage and rise above these contexts; in short, it seeks students with particular non-cognitive strengths.

William Sedlacek, professor emeritus at the University of Maryland, has conducted decades of research on non-cognitive variables relating to student success in college, variables separate from cognitive verbal and quantitative skills measured by standardized tests. Sedlacek's (2004) research includes eight non-cognitive dimensions that predict student success:

- Positive self-concept
- Realistic self-appraisal

- Successfully working within a system
- Preference for long-term goals
- Availability of a strong support person
- Leadership experience
- Community involvement
- Knowledge acquired in a field

Sedlacek's (2004) research is borne out in experiences from colleges that have integrated his model of non-cognitive assessment into admission decision-making. Since employing non-cognitive variables, collected through "Insight" essays in the admission process, Oregon State University has reported higher retention rates (OSU Admissions Blog 2008). At DePaul University, early analyses of non-cognitive essays designed on Sedlacek's dimensions also demonstrate that these are predictive of retention and academic progress.

These non-cognitive criteria are also used by the Bill and Melinda Gates Foundation in selecting recipients of the prestigious Gates Millennium Scholarships that fully fund college for talented students. Gates programs for high school students, like the Washington State Achievers Program, have reported positive outcomes with students selected through non-cognitive variables: higher academic and community engagement, and greater aspirations for and persistence toward a four-year degree (Sedlacek 2006). The Gates Millennium Scholars Program's annual report in 2011 reveals that Millennium Scholars posted a 96 percent retention rate, 79 percent five-year graduation rate, and 90 percent six-year graduation rate—double the national rate for students in similar population groups.

Sedlacek maintains that non-cognitive assessments, such as carefully crafted essays, are useful for all students, but in particular these tools are critical for students from disadvantaged backgrounds because standardized tests may not provide a full picture of a student's potential. Research at a large Midwest public university revealed that HSGPA is the strongest cognitive predictor of first-semester grades for students with lower incoming academic preparation and that non-cognitive traits such as "realistic self-appraisal" and "successfully handling the system (racism)" are the next strongest predictors (Adebayo 2008, 21). The conclusion from this study was that "admission counselors cannot rely exclusively on cognitive variables for predicting academic success for at-risk students."

In another example, Tufts University's "Kaleidoscope" approach to evaluating applicants involves essays and other performances and products that allow the "student voice" to come through. Tufts essay questions are based on a theory of intelligence that indicates abilities to succeed in life espoused by Robert Sternberg, another prominent researcher of non-cognitive indicators. The optional questions in Kaleidoscope are designed to measure creative, analytical, practical, and wisdom-based skills and attitudes; students who were rated for Kaleidoscope performed better in their freshman-year grades, holding HSGPA and SAT scores constant, and also had greater leadership and cocurricular engagement. Sternberg's book, *College Admissions for the 21st Century* (2010), reviews the five-year experiment at Tufts, making clear that traditional college admission tools are incomplete if the goal is to improve college success outcomes.

So, if it is increasingly clear from these and other studies (Dayton 2012; DeAngelo et al. 2011; Duckworth et al. 2007) that students' success in college is dependent upon a wider range of traits than is considered in the traditional admission process, a focus on expanding the admission process to include more emphasis on students' non-cognitive strengths becomes part of a retention strategy. By incorporating into the admission review process additional information that goes beyond the usual ACT or SAT scores and HSGPA, opportunities are provided for students who show academic promise but who also, on the basis of traditional admission measures, may otherwise not be admitted. When students' responses to sociological factors are acknowledged and given weight, the class profile shifts in ways that foster retention as well as other enrollment goals.

Institutional Interactions for Creating Non-Traditional Pathways

Thresher's (1966) third point asserts that admission is a reflection of institutional interactions taking place across the diverse landscape of American education. Admissions professionals have the opportunity to gaze beyond their own door and assess how their processes lead to either productive or reductive interactions with schools from kindergarten through the twelfth grade (K–12) and other colleges and universities. Can the system composed of diverse institutions do better in sorting students for outcomes such as degree completion? Can admission policies overtly recognize students' non-traditional pathways in postsecondary education and use this variance for creating innovative programs?

For example, when a profile-oriented approach to retention elevates the focus on high school curriculum and performance, then students coming from programs such as the International Baccalaureate (IB) Diploma Programme are highly desirable. These students tend to have very high retention and graduation rates in college because they are so well prepared coming in the door. Yet, when judged by college entrance test scores, many IB students do not have scores that seem admissible at selective four-year institutions; hence even highly successful students do not apply to selective colleges. These students are more likely to come from poorer families and communities and still face distinctive challenges in navigating the road to college, especially to a four-year college (Roderick et al. 2009). By explicitly acknowledging the value of the distinctive strengths of such high school curricula, colleges support what is truly important in K–12 education— learning core subject matter.

Another way for colleges to collaborate with K–12 systems is through dual enrollment programs, in which students earn college credit while still in high school. Dual enrollment incentivizes students to complete high school and enroll in a four-year college, and leads to higher retention, college GPAs, and credits earned among participants—even for students who are underrepresented and underachieving in higher education (Hughes et al. 2012; Redden 2007).

Another retention-oriented approach is to include transfer students in the overall enrollment strategy, expanding the view of profile to all students on campus, not just first-time full-time freshmen. An intentional transfer pipeline strategy is critical to the institution's overall completion rate—a metric that is being developed by the U.S. Department of Education to better reflect student outcomes for those who pursue their education in multiple settings. Transfer students may not have had exemplary high school credentials or test scores, yet bring demonstrated achievement in college courses from another institutional context. Although retention and graduation data on transfer students is not abundant, some institutions realize high rates of success with transfers. For example, at DePaul University, graduation rates for transfer students from community colleges who come in with at least one year of credits are higher than the rates for students who enter the university as freshmen. When an institution's enrollment strategy expands beyond first-time full-time freshmen (those students who are counted in current government statistics and rankings formulae), a wider array of pathways to degree can be constructed that embrace the changing college enrollment patterns of students (Borden 2004; Hossler et al. 2012) and simultaneously balance tensions between admission and retention goals. When institutions promote dual enrollment programs, carefully articulated transfer and reverse-transfer programs between community colleges and four-year universities, and institutional partnerships that reduce time to degree by eliminating redundancies or streamlining entrance to graduate programs, retention and degree completion are enhanced for the participating colleges and universities. Institutions win, students win, and the educational system wins when strategic collaborations are pursued, rather than when the players engage in all-out competition. Expanding considerations of profile to a broader group of students, who may be either concurrently enrolled or welcomed at a later time, changes the relationship of the institution to schools in K–12 settings as well as to other colleges and peers. Innovation in higher education must respond to diverse pathways that students are already choosing; retention and attainment must be defined by different metrics than what we now use.

Given the advantages of non-traditional pathways to degree completion, some might ask, "Why have institutions hesitated in shifting their admission paradigms beyond traditional selectivity measures such as test scores?" The fact remains that many university stakeholders push for increased selectivity to improve the "academic standing" or prestige of the institution, and it is an easy way to boost retention. This pursuit of selectivity is fueled by a rankings industry that circuitously equates test scores with institutional quality. So great is the perceived importance of moving up in the rankings that institutions change their behavior, their values, and even their data to play the rankings game. And the market does indeed respond accordingly, ascribing value to such rankings and the criteria they use.

A focus on prestige or rankings may also blind institutions to the value of collaborating with other institutions on a lower or higher rung of selectivity. Rather than attempt to change their current market position, an institution can think about how to create degree pathways that leverage their existing position in the higher education landscape and broaden the notion of student profile beyond first-time full-time freshmen. For example:

- San Diego State University (SDSU; n.d.) created the Compact for Success program with the local Sweetwater High School District, an initiative that guarantees admission to any student in the district who needs no remedial courses. As part of the program, SDSU faculty members meet with Sweetwater teachers to suggest changes to the high school curriculum in math and English so that more students are ready for college-level work. This program has been highly successful; SDSU four-year and six-year graduation rates showed marked improvement in the last decade.
- At the University of Central Florida (UCF; n.d.), transfer students from consortium community and state colleges are welcomed into the Direct Connect program. The program guarantees admission to UCF, providing access for students to fully accredited, flexible degree programs. Along with its Orlando campus, UCF has ten regional campus locations that provide students a variety of options for course enrollment; additionally, there are many online options available. Direct Connect students receive intensive on-site advising and curricular consultation from both community and state college advisors as well as UCF advisors. UCF retention and six-year graduation rates have increased significantly in the last decade.
- Several statewide systems are pushing for four-year institutions to award an associate degree to students who have completed the necessary requirements. "Reverse-transfer" agreements are being intentionally crafted in states such as Hawaii, Maryland, Texas, Tennessee, and New Hampshire and are seen as an alternative pathway to awarding a credential to students on the way to a bachelor's degree (Fain 2012).

Conclusion

Test-optional policies, admission practices that incorporate non-cognitive factors, and innovative enrollment pathways are at the leading edge of national trends and can be considered viable retention strategies. For the vast number of institutions, described by Kalsbeek and Zucker in chapter 2 as the middle market based on Zemsky, Shaman, and Iannozzi's (1997) well-known diagram of the higher education market, test-optional, non-cognitive approaches and intentional collaborations can be a win-win scenario for students and institutional retention rates. These institutions have the opportunity to design admission practices that serve the public interest by improving both degree completion for a broad group of students and institutional metrics of retention and completion.

A 2011 survey conducted by Inside Higher Ed revealed that 40 percent of admissions directors at four-year institutions are expanding the use of non-traditional factors in making admission decisions and that 28 percent of admissions directors reported a reduction in the weight of standardized tests among factors for admission (Jasick 2011). Higher education news is reporting with increasing frequency on new degree-pathway programs being developed between institutions or within statewide systems. Admissions professionals are responding by broadening the concept of who makes up the student profile and what characteristics are important.

Thresher knew back in 1966 that innovation and change to an institution's profile is possible:

> As entrance requirements in the older sense have diminished in importance, efforts have increased to select students on broad grounds of intellectual promise and aptitude, to understand the dynamics of personality as it affects motives and energy, and to trace the dimensions of human excellence beyond such deceptively simple, unidimensional quantities as school marks and test scores. (5)

As both the nation and specific institutions seek improved retention and degree-completion outcomes, all would do well to keep this eloquent assertion in mind.

References

Adebayo, B. 2008. "Cognitive and Non-Cognitive Factors: Affecting the Academic Performance and Retention of Conditionally Admitted Freshmen." *Journal of College Admission*, no. 200:15–21.

Atkinson, R., and S. Geiser. 2012. "Reflections on a Century of College Admissions Tests." In *SAT Wars: The Case for Test-Optional College Admissions*, edited by J. A. Soares, 23–49. New York: Teachers College Press, Columbia University.

Balmer, S. 2012, May. *Dickinson: Test-Optional Admission Policy [PowerPoint slides]*. Presentation at the annual conference of the Illinois Association of College Admission Counselors, Itasca.

Borden, V. M. H. 2004. "Accommodating Student Swirl: When Traditional Students Are No Longer the Tradition." *Change* 36(2):10–16.

Bowen, W. G., and D. Bok. 1998. *The Shape of the River: Long-Term Consequences of Considering Race in College and University Admissions*. Princeton, N.J.: Princeton University Press.

Bowen, W. G., M. M. Chingos, and M. S. McPherson. 2009. *Crossing the Finish Line: Completing College at America's Public Universities*. Princeton, N.J.: Princeton University Press.

Camara, W., and G. Echternacht. 2000. *The SAT I and High School Grades: Utility in Predicting Success in College* (College Board Report No. RN–10). New York: College Entrance Examination Board.

Cortes, C., and C. Klaas. 2011, September. *DePaul's Test-Optional Decision: A Student-Centered Approach [PowerPoint slides]*. Presentation at the annual conference of the National Association for College Admission Counseling (NACAC), New Orleans.

Dayton, E. 2012. "First in My Family: Family Relationships and Educational Mobility." PhD diss., Johns Hopkins University.

DeAngelo, L., R. Franke, S. Hurtado, J. H. Pryor, and S. Tran. 2011. *Completing College: Assessing Graduation Rates at Four-Year Institutions*. Los Angeles: Higher Education Research Institute, University of California, Los Angeles.

Duckworth, A., C. Peterson, M. D. Matthews, and D. R. Kelly. 2007. "Grit: Perseverance and Passion for Long-Term Goals." *Journal of Personality and Social Psychology* 101(6):1317–31.

Epstein, J. P. 2009. "Behind the SAT-Optional Movement: Context and Controversy." *Journal of College Admission*, no. 204:8–19.

Fain, P. 2012. "Common Sense on Completion." Accessed September 3, 2012, http://www.insidehighered.com/news/2012/05/23/statewide-reverse-transfer-catches-could-boost-graduation-rates.

Gates Millennium Scholars Program. 2011. "Moving Forward by Giving Back: 2011 Annual Report." Fairfax, Va.: United Negro College Fund.

Geiser, S., and M. Santelices. 2007. "Validity of High School Grades in Predicting Student Success Beyond the Freshman Year: High School Record vs. Standardized Tests as Indicators of Four-Year College Outcomes." Berkeley: Center for Studies in Higher Education, University of California.

Hossler, D., D. Shapiro, A. Dundar, M. Ziskin, D. Zerquera, and V. Torres. 2012. *Transfer and Mobility: A National View of Pre-Degree Student Movement in Postsecondary Institutions*. Bloomington, Ind.: National Student Clearinghouse Research Center.

Hughes, K. L., O. Rodriguez, L. Edwards, and C. Belfield. 2012. *Broadening the Benefits of Dual Enrollment Reaching Underachieving and Underrepresented Students with Career-Focused Programs*. New York: Community College Research Center, Columbia University.

Jasick, S. 2011. "Clashes of Money and Values: A Survey of Admissions Directors." Accessed September 3, 2012, http://www.insidehighered.com/news/survey/admissions2011.

Kalsbeek, D. H., and Associates. 2009, May. "Undergraduate Retention and Degree Completion: Exploring the Relationship of Academic Preparation, Performance and Progress, with Financial Need and Financial Aid on Retention and Degree Completion." Paper presented to the DePaul University Board of Trustees, Chicago.

Kobrin, J. L., B. F. Patterson, E. J. Shaw, K. D. Mattern, and S. M. Barbuti. 2008. "Validity of the SAT for Predicting First-Year College Grade Point Average." College Board Research Report, No. 2008-5. New York: The College Board.

Lovett, C. M. 2005. "The Perils of Pursuing Prestige." *The Chronicle of Higher Education Review* 51(20):B20.

Lydon, C. 2012, May. *Test-Optional Admission at Providence College [PowerPoint slides]*. Presentation at the annual conference of the Illinois Association of College Admission Counselors, Itasca.

Nankervis, B. 2011. "Gender Inequities in College Admission Due to the Differential Validity of the SAT." *Journal of College Admission*, no. 213:24–30.

National Association for College Admission Counseling. 2008. *Report of the Commission on the Use of Standardized Tests in Undergraduate Admission*. Arlington, Va.: National Association for College Admission Counseling.

OSU Admissions Blog. 2008. "The Times They are a Changin'." Accessed September 22, 2012, http://oregonstate.edu/admissions/blog/2008/10/05/the-times-they-are-a-changin/.

Redden, E. 2007. "The Benefits of Dual Enrollment." Accessed September 3, 2012, http://www.insidehighered.com/news/2007/10/17/dualenroll.

Roderick, M., J. Nagaoka, V. Coca, and E. Moeller. 2009. "From High School to the Future: Making Hard Work Pay Off." Chicago: The University of Chicago Consortium on Chicago School Research.

San Diego State University. n.d. "Compact for Success." Accessed September 3, 2012, http://newscenter.sdsu.edu/compact/Default.aspx.

Schmidt, P. 2008. "Most Colleges Chase Prestige on a Treadmill, Researchers Find." *The Chronicle of Higher Education* 55(13):A14.

Sedlacek, W. E. 2004. *Beyond the Big Test: Noncognitive Assessment in Higher Education.* San Francisco: Jossey-Bass.

Sedlacek, W. E. 2006, November. *Gates Millennium Scholars & Washington State Achievers: The Role of Private Scholarship Programs in College Enrollment [PowerPoint slides].* Presentation at the Sixteenth Annual Strategic Enrollment Management (SEM XVI) Conference, Phoenix.

Shanley, B. J. 2007. "Test-Optional Admission at a Liberal Arts College: A Founding Mission Affirmed." *Harvard Educational Review* 77(4):429–34.

Soares, J. A., ed. 2012. *SAT Wars: The Case for Test-Optional Admissions.* New York: Teachers College Press, Columbia University.

Sternberg, R. 2010. *College Admissions for the 21st Century.* Cambridge, Mass.: Harvard University Press.

Thresher, B. A. 1966. *College Admission and the Public Interest.* New York: The College Entrance Examination Board.

University of Central Florida. n.d. "Direct Connect to UCF." Accessed September 3, 2012, http://regionalcampuses.ucf.edu/directconnect.

Zemsky, R., S. Shaman, and M. Iannozzi. 1997. "In Search of a Strategic Perspective: A Tool for Mapping the Market in Post-Secondary Education." *Change* 29(6):23–38.

Zwick, R. 2007. "College Admission Testing." Arlington, Va.: National Association for College Admission Counseling.

CARLA M. CORTES *is the retention project leader for the division of Enrollment Management and Marketing at DePaul University.*

7

This chapter offers several principles and institutional examples of the ways that student-centered process- and progress-related improvements enhance students' experiences and outcomes.

Process and Progress in Action: Examples of What Works

Charles C. Schroeder

As argued earlier in this text, focusing on the student experience broadly defined and, in particular, on the quality of student encounters in and out of the classroom is of critical importance to improving student outcomes. Improving learning, satisfaction, retention, time to degree, and graduation outcomes is not predicated simply on improving entering characteristics or adding institutional resources, but rather on how student services are integrated and whether supportive resources are deployed in ways that motivate and inspire students to effectively engage with them. This chapter offers several principles to consider and several institutional examples of how improvements in selected processes can enhance students' experiences and outcomes by ensuring that the processes are more student-centered and more focused on ensuring student progress toward degree completion.

Improving the Consistency, Quality, and Effectiveness of Institutional Services

To be successful, students must interact effectively with a range of services at appropriate times throughout their undergraduate years. These include negotiating the enrollment process, which involves admission, financial aid, advising, registration, student accounts, etc., as well as entities such as the bookstore, dining services, parking, and transportation. Unfortunately, many of these interactions are anything but seamless and satisfying; in fact, they are often uncoordinated and dysfunctional. How common, for example, is the following scenario? A student may be unaware of a hold on her registration because of a $5 library fine or a $15 parking ticket; she meets with her advisor, agrees on a schedule, and proceeds to registration only to

NEW DIRECTIONS FOR HIGHER EDUCATION, no. 161, Spring 2013 © Wiley Periodicals, Inc.
Published online in Wiley Online Library (wileyonlinelibrary.com) • DOI:10.1002/he.20047

learn that her access has been blocked due to the holds. After paying the fees, the student returns to register and finds that two of her five desired courses have already filled. As a result, she now must return to her advisor and reinitiate the process. This is but one example of typical dysfunctional and inefficient registration processes that produce waste rather than value. It is also an example of a significant disconnect between students' initial institutional service expectations and actual experiences often created through the admission process. The greater the incongruence between students' expectations for fairness and responsiveness and existing administrative practices and processes, the greater the likelihood that students will become disenchanted and choose to leave the college or university (Braxton and Hirschy 2005).

Most institutions have to overcome four major barriers if they want to improve the quality and consistency of their services. These barriers are:

1. Major processes are segregated. Units operate in relative isolation from one another.
2. Systems are not integrated. Staff members focus on their narrow set of responsibilities and disregard the interconnected nature of the process they are a part of.
3. While vertical communication may be adequate, horizontal communication is usually extremely limited.
4. Administrative functions are not linked and aligned. Units focus quite naturally on their functional responsibilities while neglecting a systemic orientation that requires functional integration and synergy.

What is needed to reduce or erase these barriers is a compelling, unifying institutional commitment to campuswide service excellence. For schools that have embarked on this quest, the first step is often to create an institutional service strategy or pledge such as: "Service to our students and other customers will be fast, friendly, effective, simple, and flexible." This seeks to accomplish the following objectives: (a) it serves as a clear aim that focuses staff efforts on the elements of the pledge; (b) it demonstrates staff members' commitment to one another and their internal and external customers; (c) it provides common ground for collective effort; (d) it creates the platform for continuous improvement based upon clear and measurable service standards; and, most importantly, (e) the strategy makes explicit the institutions' commitment to being student-centered and success-oriented. The keys to the success of such a strategy are having staff members define in behavioral and measurable terms the meaning of "fast," "friendly," "effective," etc., and encouraging them to create assessment tools, such as "mystery shopper" programs, to gather and utilize systematic and relevant data and feedback loops for continuous improvement purposes (Schroeder 2001). Such a strategy communicates in a very clear and concise manner to all students that "you matter to us." And, as the research indicates, schools with high levels of student satisfaction enjoy much higher graduation and alumni giving rates (Schreiner 2009).

An orientation to service excellence in creating student-centered processes requires identifying the primary beneficiaries of the service and then being brutally honest about the effectiveness and efficiency of service delivery. When it comes to enhancing student success, many areas of the student experience lend themselves to major review and subsequent improvement. The following institutional examples illustrate the central importance of shifting the focus from being "staff-centered" to being "student-centered" when improving institutional processes.

Overcoming Dysfunctional Business Processes. At the University of Missouri–Columbia (MU), the loan disbursement process involves three primary units: financial aid, the cashier's office, and the University system central office. Countless students complained that after filing their financial aid forms, they waited for more than two months to receive their checks. As a result, they had to take out emergency loans in order to clear their accounts before being permitted to register for classes. Hence, poor "hand-offs" between these offices adversely affected the advising, course selection, and registration functions. Interestingly, this problem had existed for more than two decades with staff members in the three offices routinely blaming others for the problems. Over time, these individuals had become "functionally nearsighted"; that is, they focused only on their positions and demonstrated little responsibility for results produced by the process. In addition, they were fixated on short-term events—immediately responding to problems, packaging aid, completing daily reports, and so forth—and were unable to see how their actions extended beyond the boundaries of their positions. Metaphorically, staff could easily see their individual trees, but didn't recognize the relationship between them and the forest. Fortunately, this story had a happy ending. Directors from the three offices agreed to form a cross-functional team whose members subsequently received training in process analysis and redesign. After analyzing each step in the loan disbursement process—from the initial submission of the aid form to the receipt of the check—and determining if each step added value or simply produced waste, the team reduced a 67-day process to 19 days. This change improved institutional cash flow, eliminated emergency loans by 70 percent, and reduced staff by the equivalent of three full-time positions—a win-win situation for everyone.

Eliminating Frustrating Bottlenecks. Bottlenecks are a type of "waste" that can take many forms, but the most common manifestation is long lines, usually in a variety of institutional service areas such as bookstores. Students on every campus must interact with their campus bookstore throughout the academic year and as a result often find that buying books at the start of each semester can be an onerous, time-consuming, and exceedingly frustrating process. Why? Usually because of long lines that may extend beyond the boundaries of the stores. Some bookstores, such as the one at MU, have recognized this problem as an opportunity to improve their services by "thinking outside the box." Instead of the customary approach of adding more personnel and cash registers (i.e., overhead), the MU store encouraged first-year students during summer orientation to place orders for their books and supplies before departing for home. Once the orders were received, the staff individually boxed the desired items, charged the appropriate student accounts, and delivered the boxes to the appropriate rooms in each of the residence halls one day before students arrived. This innovative solution to overcoming major bottlenecks was another example of a process improvement and a win-win situation for everyone—students got what they needed in a seamless, responsive manner, and the bookstore freed up space for the sale of higher margin items such as memorabilia and branded merchandise.

Reducing Service Problems Through Proactive Strategies. Staff members in the financial aid office at the University of Arizona were always anxious just before financial aid letters were mailed to new students. Within a few days of the mailing, the phone lines and email systems were literally overwhelmed with inquiries. It appears that students and parents alike could not decipher their award letters. Although the financial aid office distributed elaborate and expensive financial aid guidebooks during the recruitment process, recipients either didn't read them or simply couldn't understand financial aid basics. As part of a service-excellence audit, staff members were asked to list the top ten questions parents and students routinely asked when they called or emailed the offices. Interestingly, the "top ten" were basically the same questions year after year! Since the office had historically recorded on an hourly basis the number of calls and emails, annual baseline data were readily available. The school engaged a quality consultant who suggested a proactive strategy for reducing inquiries, streamlining processes, and improving customer and staff satisfaction. Here's how the new approach was implemented. Prior to the distribution of the award letters, students and parents would receive a letter along with a one-page document that listed the top ten financial aid questions along with the answers. After initiating this strategy, data on incoming calls and emails were benchmarked against the average numbers during the same time periods in previous years. The improvements were dramatic and impressive—calls and emails were reduced more than 65 percent, thereby resulting in substantial increases in effectiveness, efficiency, satisfaction, and staff morale. Perhaps most importantly, however, staff members in the office came to the realization that their primary mission was not simply the packaging and distribution of financial aid, but rather facilitating higher levels of student success by making a collegiate education accessible and affordable.

Improving Course Availability and Scheduling. With college costs rising at alarming rates, institutions are under increased pressure to graduate students in four rather than six years. There are many factors associated with time to degree, but one of the most important, yet least emphasized, is course availability and scheduling. Many institutions have struggled to address these issues. At Lynchburg College, Baylor University, and Seattle University, for example, the first step to improvement involved completing a comprehensive classroom utilization study that revealed excess capacity early in the morning and from mid-afternoon on. Each of these institutions improved time to degree by initiating the following changes: (a) Lynchburg scheduled each student class cohort (freshmen, sophomores, etc.) for the entire academic year rather than on a semester-by-semester basis; (b) Baylor— where various colleges and schools "owned their space" that other units could not utilize, even when excess capacity occurred—permitted colleges and schools five days to schedule their own classroom space, and after this timeframe, unassigned space was made available to anyone needing it; (c) Seattle University created a highly innovative "Core Solution Center" that provides quick and responsive support during registration periods by having advising staff available to help students resolve closed classes and scheduling issues; (d) all three institutions used sophisticated flow-through models to anticipate curriculum needs for each class by major and program areas, which enables the provision of adequate sections in advance of registration; and, (e) while all three originally identified parking as their number one student problem, after completing a classroom utilization study, they all realized that the "parking problem" was in fact a course scheduling/ utilization problem. That is, by historically scheduling the majority of classes from 10 a.m. to 2 p.m., these institutions had unintentionally created a compression effect where almost everyone was on campus at the same time. By creating more equitable, student-centered scheduling policies and practices, they not only improved time to degree and reduced costs for students, they also solved their number one problem—parking!

Other Examples of Fostering Student Progress Through Process Improvements

The following are additional examples of how student progress and outcomes are improved by focusing on process improvements.

Improving Success Rates in High-Risk Courses. One of the greatest barriers to progress, and hence graduation, is unacceptable academic performance during the first college year. In fact, as much as 50 percent of fall-to-fall attrition is associated with students who are placed on academic probation, usually because of failure in required courses. One of the best predictors of attrition is poor performance in initial math courses. In community colleges, for example, 50 percent of entering students fail their first math course and the same percent fail again when repeating it (Tagg 2003). At Bowling Green State University, 49 percent ($N = 810$) of first-year students in 27 fall-semester sections of college algebra failed the course, and many of these students were placed on academic probation. Similarly, of the

627 freshmen at Baylor University enrolled in various spring semester Math 1300 courses (a gateway course required for entry into specific programs and schools), 106 received a grade of D or F, and 96 of them did not return for their sophomore year.

Researchers at Indiana University–Bloomington discovered patterns similar to those at Bowling Green and Baylor. Through systematic assessment, Hossler, Kuh, and Olsen (2001) determined that almost 40 percent of students who enrolled in gateway mathematics courses, such as M118 (finite math), received a D- or F grade or withdrew from the class. Because the class is required for other majors, it became the catalyst for developing a partnership between enrollment services and the math department to improve student performance and educational attainment. The primary initiative was the development of a two-semester, reduced-pace equivalent of M118. Students were advised to register for reduced-pace sections both before the semester and after it began. This allowed students whose performance seemed likely to result in a D or F final grade to fall back to the reduced-pace course and master the complicated concepts of finite mathematics in a more manageable timeframe.

In addition, a cross-functional team developed an extremely innovative, interactive television supplement, *The Finite Show*, which was produced to appeal to the media-oriented undergraduates, most of whom have nocturnal study habits. The show, which airs Monday through Thursday evenings over the campus cable system, is hosted by an accomplished M118 instructor and guest lecturers and uses a combination of problem solving and live calls from students. *The Finite Show* is available in all residence hall rooms as well as off-campus living arrangements. These innovative interventions substantially enhanced first-year student performance: 90 percent of the students in the two-semester, reduced-pace sequence achieved a grade of C or better, and similar results have been recorded for students who viewed *The Finite Show* on a regular basis (Schroeder 2005).

Creating Early Identification/Intervention Programs. As emphasized in chapter 1, the academic profile of the entering class is an excellent predictor of subsequent success. Most institutions use some form of an academic index score to profile the characteristics of entering students, and, not surprisingly, students in the lower quintiles and quartiles persist and graduate at significantly lower rates. Since most campuses cannot substantially improve their academic profile, they must find ways to increase the learning productivity of underprepared and underperforming students. Lynchburg College, for example, uses a five-tier academic index score from A (highest ability) to E (lowest ability). When the school's fall-to-fall retention rate unexpectedly dropped from 71 to 66 percent, not surprisingly, most of the attrition occurred in level D and E students. Many of these students received no institutional grant aid and hence accounted for a significant portion of much needed net revenue. At the request of Lynchburg's president, a student success team was created, which focused on improving the academic performance of these students by using the following strategies: implementation of intrusive and ongoing academic advising, calibration of course schedules, early monitoring of progress, immediate faculty electronic referrals for underperformance, and robust academic coaching. The results were remarkable. In one year, the retention rates for D and E students improved 32 and 28 percent, respectively, and these increases enabled the college to attain its five-year retention goal of 75 percent in only one year. In addition, the graduation rate for this at-risk cohort was 61.5 percent, a gain of 3.5 percent from the prior year. Since implementing the program for at-risk D and E students, Lynchburg has recorded annual increases in these academic index groups' graduation rates of 5 to 6 percent (Normyle 2011).

Configuring Facilities to Optimize Coordination and Integration of Academic Support and Enrichment Services. Campuses across the country have come to realize that they cannot improve graduation rates without substantially reducing attrition in the first two years of college. And they have found that simply adding resources to highly fragmented, compartmentalized, and uncoordinated programs does not achieve the progress and progression objectives they seek to attain. To address these challenges, many schools have created comprehensive, integrated, and service-oriented student success centers that link and align existing units such as academic advising, educational support services, career development, minority student programs, counseling, and first- to second-year experiences in one conveniently located, easily accessible facility. Effective examples include Baylor University's Paul Foster Student Success Center and similar centers at MU and Auburn University. All of these institutions report that their centers have contributed to increases in retention and graduation rates. In addition, other large universities, such as Indiana University–Bloomington and Bowling Green State University, have created decentralized "satellite" student success centers in strategically located geographic areas of the campus, such as large residential complexes, libraries, and student unions, thereby providing easily accessible and convenient academic services to a range of students.

It is important to emphasize, however, that simply placing units with similar and complementary missions under the same roof does not necessarily enhance student success. The units might still maintain a compartmentalized, silo mentality. Leaders at Auburn University addressed this challenge by utilizing twenty cross-functional teams to better understand the nature of their students' experiences. Their exploration discovered that "the method of service delivery has required a paradigm shift. Units historically responsible for delivering focused services are now required to address the 'whole' student, taking into consideration transitional, academic, personal, and career needs" (McDaniel, James, and Davis 2000, 28).

Creating Clear Pathways to Student Success

The literature on educational attainment consistently underscores the importance of high expectations for student success (Blimling and Whitt 1993; Chickering and Gamson 1987; Kuh et al. 2005; Pascarella and Terenzini 2005). Unfortunately, expectations for effort are rarely included in marketing materials, emphasized during orientation, and reinforced in first-year classes. In addition, students are usually the only ones on campus who do not have a "job description," and they do not have clear maps directing them to educational experiences that can enhance their chances of degree completion (Schilling and Schilling 1999).

As part of a substantial reform of undergraduate education at the University of Kansas (KU), the institution chose to focus primarily on increasing graduation rates by emphasizing the critical importance of students' involvement in educationally purposeful experiences throughout their undergraduate experience. New students are introduced during summer orientation to the importance of graduating by participating in traditions and rituals and through the necessity of using their "Graduate in Four" educational planning notebook. The notebook provides students with information about how to make the most of each of their undergraduate years and what they need to do to complete their degree program in a timely manner. It encourages them to meet academic expectations for success and to select high impact out-of-class activities that can enrich their undergraduate experience. In addition, the notebook includes sections for each of the four undergraduate years along with a "checklist" that students use to determine whether they are making appropriate choices. The notebook is utilized in the required University 101 freshman seminar, and students must take it to every advising session that occurs in the Freshman-Sophomore Advising Center (FSAC). The notebook helps students, as well as staff, map and monitor whether they are making appropriate progress toward the completion of a degree (Kuh et al. 2005).

KU also sponsors a unique and powerful tradition that symbolically and substantively underscores the overarching importance of graduation. The highest point on the KU campus is the Memorial Campanile. It is a well accepted tradition that no undergraduate can walk under the Campanile until graduation day, when members of the senior class line up and march through the Campanile to the stadium where they receive their degrees. This rite of passage and literal "pathway" are constant reminders of one of KU's most important institutional aspirations and goals—graduation!

Lessons in Efforts to Improve Time to Degree and Completion Rates

While the previously shared examples cover a variety of institutional improvements, they reflect similar principles and perspectives that can serve as lessons for guiding future efforts to improve retention, progression, and graduation rates. These include the following:

Create a Compelling Aim and Champion its Attainment. A compelling aim directs attention on what matters most to institutional vitality. In the case of many of the institutions highlighted in this chapter, senior leaders championed the importance of performance improvement and the centrality of improving graduation rates as a primary metric. In some cases, leaders used state mandates and declining net revenue as "triggering events" to mobilize understanding and impel action. Crafting clear and explicit aims and advocating and championing their attainment are the critical first steps in increasing graduation rates through improving the undergraduate experience.

Challenge Prevailing Assumptions, and Think and Act Systemically. Adopting an organizational learning and improvement orientation requires thinking outside the box. Who, for example, would consider using a campus television channel to improve performance in gateway math courses, or delivering textbooks to students' residence hall rooms before they check in? Or how common is it for faculty and academic administrators and, for that matter, student affairs staffs to believe that residence halls should be intentional locales for student learning that foster success in general education courses? Thinking and acting systemically requires understanding the differences between organizational functions and processes. Creating systems that promote performance improvement requires crossing organizational and disciplinary boundaries to connect, link, and align people, resources, and concepts to produce mutually valued outcomes.

Foster Shared Institutional Responsibility for Educational Quality and Student Success. Shifting from a functional silo to functional alignment and integration mentality can only be achieved by emphasizing the centrality of cooperation and collaboration. Until key institutional agents and agencies understand the important contributions they can make to student success and how, in turn, they benefit from engaging in an improvement effort, it will be difficult, if not impossible, to foster shared responsibility.

Conclusion

For far too long, institutions have assumed that creating a variety of highly specialized, narrowly tailored, boutique programs for small cohorts of students is the key to enhancing retention and graduation rates. While some programs of this nature do add value, the highly effective colleges and universities featured in this chapter have embraced a different approach by instead recognizing that improving a few processes that touch large numbers of students in powerful ways produce the greatest and most beneficial results.

NEW DIRECTIONS FOR HIGHER EDUCATION • DOI:10.1002/he

References

Blimling, G., and E. Whitt, eds. 1993. *Good Practice in Student Affairs: Principles to Foster Student Learning*. San Francisco: Jossey-Bass.

Braxton, J. M., and A. S. Hirschy. 2005. "Theoretical Developments in the Study of College Student Departure." In *College Student Retention: Formula for Success*, edited by A. Seidman, 61–87. Westport, Conn.: American Council on Education and Praeger Publishing.

Chickering, A. W., and Z. F. Gamson. 1987. "Seven Principles for Good Practice in Undergraduate Education." *AAHE Bulletin* 39(7):3–7.

Hossler, D., G. D. Kuh, and D. Olsen. 2001. "Finding Fruit on the Vine: Using Higher Education Research and Institutional Research to Guide Institutional Policies and Strategies (Part II)." *Research in Higher Education* 42:223–235.

Kuh, G. D., J. Kinzie, J. H. Schuh, E. J. Whitt, and Associates. 2005. *Student Success in College: Creating Conditions That Matter*. San Francisco: Jossey-Bass.

McDaniel, N., J. B. James, and G. Davis. 2000. "The Student Success Center at Auburn University." *About Campus* 5(1):25–28.

Normyle, M. 2011. "Male College Students and Success: A Study of Early Predictors of Academic Performance, Progression, and Persistence of Male Undergraduate Students." PhD diss., University of Virginia.

Pascarella, E. T., and P. T. Terenzini. 2005. *How College Affects Students: A Third Decade of Research*, vol. 2. San Francisco: Jossey-Bass.

Schilling, K. M., and K. L. Schilling. 1999. "Increasing Expectations for Student Effort." *About Campus* 4(2):4–10.

Schreiner, L. A. 2009. *Linking Student Satisfaction and Retention*. Iowa City: Noel-Levitz.

Schroeder, C. C. 2001. "The Mystery Shopper Program: An Innovative Tool for Assessing Performance." In *Proving and Improving: Strategies for Assessing the First College Year*, edited by R. L. Swing, 75–78. Columbia: University of South Carolina, National Resource Center for the First-Year Experience and Students in Transition.

Schroeder, C. C. 2005. "Collaborative Partnerships Between Academic and Student Affairs." In *Challenging & Supporting the First-Year Student: A Handbook for Improving the First Year of College*, edited by M. L. Upcraft, J. N. Gardner, and B. O. Barefoot, 204–220. San Francisco: Jossey-Bass.

Tagg, J. 2003. *The Learning Paradigm College*. Bolton, Mass.: Anker Publishing.

CHARLES C. SCHROEDER is a senior associate consultant for Noel-Levitz, specializing in retention and student success strategies and interventions.

This chapter highlights institutional examples of intentional approaches to ensuring that every student's experience reflects the promise of the institutional brand or mission as well as the distinct and differentiating nature of the institution's educational philosophy and purpose.

Promise in Action: Examples of Institutional Success

George D. Kuh

"For what shall this institution be known?"

I often pose that question when visiting campuses seeking ways to enhance student accomplishment and success. The question is intended to spur thinking about whether the institution has fulfilled its purpose and brand promise around distinctive or special attributes and opportunities. What sets it apart from others with a similar mission, location, or denominational affiliation, or comparable size? To push further, I might ask:

> "If I were to meet one of your recent graduates on the street in London, Johannesburg, Seoul, or Seattle, how would I know from hearing about their college experience and their views on social and global issues that they graduated from here? Put another way, what is the imprint this place leaves on those who have studied here?"

In this era of mass higher education, with institutions enrolling tens of thousands of students and distance learning on the rise, it sounds almost quaint, perhaps naïve to ponder not just whether but how a college could arrange its curricular and cocurricular programs and experiences in order to intentionally cultivate in its graduates a distinctive constellation of knowledge, abilities, dispositions, and values.

Yet that is what this volume is suggesting we do. Is this idea realistic and attainable? Or is it an idealized, nostalgic notion of the way colleges were thought to be at some earlier point in history, when the curriculum was more or less prescribed and students were of similar age and essentially a captive audience, living in close proximity to one another and their teachers? In the changing landscape of higher education, can large complex institutions serving diverse populations of both residential and

NEW DIRECTIONS FOR HIGHER EDUCATION, no. 161, Spring 2013 © Wiley Periodicals, Inc.
Published online in Wiley Online Library (wileyonlinelibrary.com) • DOI:10.1002/he.20048

non-traditional commuting students achieve this ideal through a mix of learning approaches?

This book's opening chapter challenges us to marry strategic efforts to improve student success and institutional effectiveness with the institution's brand research and brand development efforts. While the institutional mission informs and sustains the brand, the two are not interchangeable. In pursuit of the latter, effective messaging and marketing convey to students what differentiates the institution from other possible choices—the promise made. Institutions seek to touch all students in deep, personally meaningful ways consistent with the institution's educational mission and philosophy so that when they graduate they are well on their way to developing an informed view of the world and their place in it.

Therefore, do students arrive with expectations about the nature and depth of their educational experience at their chosen college? Do students graduate, having been satisfied that their expectations were met or exceeded, setting the stage for a lifelong bond with the institution?

One way to approximate an answer to these questions is to draw heavily on historical accounts and complementary educational philosophies and pedagogical approaches that—if implemented at a high level of quality—should, in theory, resemble the kind of learning ecosystem that a 4 Ps framework imagines. Another way is to offer working examples of institutions that seem to have proven that what this framework poses is possible and desirable.

In this chapter, I take the second path, which occasionally intersects with the first. That is, I will illustrate how three campuses have, in their own way, attempted to bring coherence to the student experience and enrich that experience by more closely matching what was promised to what each student actually experiences while enrolled. Fulfilling students' expectations that were purposefully articulated in the mission and thoughtfully created through the brand is the objective.

In the end, these examples do not stand as roadmaps to institutional transformation. A small book would be needed to adequately describe how these colleges and universities revised their academic programs and shaped their campus cultures to align with a higher degree of fidelity what they say they are about with what students do and experience. It is obvious that institutions are too complex to infer that what works in one setting need only be transported and adapted for a different context. Even so, reflecting on how these three schools have attempted to deliver what they promise will hopefully provoke fresh thinking that may then evolve into an idea or two for how to bring what we say is supposed to happen to our students closer to what they actually experience. In addition, the institutional examples in this chapter highlight high-impact practices (Kuh 2007, 2008, 2010)—activities that benefit students and encourage learning in unusually powerful ways—which are a means for implementing critical aspects of the institutional promise. All types of institutions can find ways to intentionally design and offer high-impact experiences to students that are coherent with their mission and brand promise.

From Promise to Practice: Examples from the Field

Valencia College. Some community colleges are meeting the challenge of making good on their promise head on. Consider Valencia College in Florida, a multi-campus institution with 50,000+ students whose mission is to provide opportunities for academic, technical, and lifelong learning in a collaborative culture dedicated to inquiry, results, and excellence. As a two-year college, Valencia began its transformation into a learning-centered institution in 1995, with a goal of "institutionalizing effective innovations and improving measurable learning outcomes" (Valencia Community College Planning Council 2004).

To this end, the institution ultimately determined what students should know or do upon program completion. Students must demonstrate through their authentic work Valencia's four Student Core Competencies and seven Program Learning Outcomes for associate degree, honors, and certificate programs. To demonstrate attainment of the Core Competencies and Program Outcomes, students are encouraged to provide samples of their work compiled in a learning portfolio.

Valencia introduced learning communities, among other support mechanisms to help students succeed, in 1996 and now has more than three dozen learning communities operating. Valencia's LinC (Learning in Communities) pairs two courses taken by the same students. Instructors sit in on each other's class and "team teach" throughout the term. As suggested in the learning communities literature, students in LinC courses build stronger relationships with peers and their teachers and are more likely to persist from semester to semester. As part of its participation in the national Achieving the Dream initiative, Valencia expanded and centralized the coordination of its learning communities by appointing a full-time college-wide LinC Coordinator.

As of Fall 2011, Valencia also awards baccalaureate degrees. The College has been recognized by various organizations for its pioneering work in maintaining a laser-like focus on learning outcomes. Granted, an inordinate amount of faculty and staff time and effort, along with a "stay the course" mandate from institutional leaders, was required. It also helped that the institution received outside support from philanthropic groups for this work. The investment by all parties proved it can be done, which makes Valencia an exemplar worth emulating. Much can also be learned from other institutions in the two-year sector that have put student success first, including El Paso Community College, Houston Community College, and LaGuardia Community College.

Luther College. Luther College is affiliated with the Evangelical Lutheran Church of America, and the College makes this affiliation clear in its mission statement and elsewhere in materials sent to prospective, current, and former students. Luther's core institutional values affirm the "liberating power of faith and learning" in a diverse community to "serve with distinction for the common good." Luther expects its 2,500 students to "understand and confront a changing society" while practicing "joyful stewardship of the resources that surround us" (Luther College 2012).

How does Luther deliver on these promises? The physical plant in Decorah, Iowa, is in harmony with its natural surroundings; campus buildings and plantings, new and old, are faithful to the master plan developed by famed landscape architect, Jens Jensen, one of the best-known proponents of the Prairie School of Design in the early 20th century. The institution's commitment to sustainability is demonstrated in word and deed. It is among the charter members of the College & University Presidents' Climate Commitment (ACUPCC), and faculty, staff, and students are asked to sign its Energy Conservation Pledge. And in Fall 2011, after a five-year effort spearheaded by faculty and students, a wind turbine was made operational on a nearby land parcel the college had obtained for that purpose.

As expected, the curriculum is another major vehicle by which the college enacts its mission with demonstrably positive effects on students. Required religion classes span a variety of denominational and faith perspectives, encouraging students to ponder the connections between religious convictions and liberal learning. And the January term makes it possible for students to experience settings very different from its rural Northeast Iowa location and apply what they are learning in a larger world off campus. Two required J-terms, one for all first-year students and another before graduation, explain in large part why 75 percent of Luther students are able to study away from campus at some point.

A major integrating mechanism is the multiple-semester Paideia Program, which blends faith and liberal arts learning. Paideia, the Greek word for education, encompasses common formal and informal learning experiences that lead to a shared worldview and includes three interdisciplinary courses: a common two-semester writing-intensive sequence for first-year students (Paideia I) and a series of one-semester courses for juniors and seniors (Paideia II).

To determine whether the combination of integrated in-class and out-of-class experiences touches students in meaningful and substantive ways, just look at the college's National Survey of Student Engagement (NSSE) results. It's no surprise, perhaps, that compared with their counterparts at other liberal arts colleges as well as larger universities, Luther students report engaging more frequently in activities that enhance their spirituality and also deepening their spiritual beliefs to a greater degree during college. At the same time, Luther students are also more likely to do a practicum or internship, study abroad, take a foreign language, and participate in a senior culminating experience. In addition, Luther's first-year retention rate is 87 percent, and its six-year graduation rate was 74 percent in 2010—5 points above the rate predicted by the 2012 *U.S. News & World Report* rankings formula. These outcomes, combined with high acceptance rates by medical, dental, and law schools; a top-ten ranking among small colleges with NCAA post-graduate scholarships; and many competitive awards suggest that Luther lives up to its promise as a place that integrates faith and learning in the context of a rigorous liberal arts curriculum.

Elon University. George Keller was a discerning, sometimes acerbically critical observer of American higher education for the last half of the 20th century. One of his last publications, in 2004, was a little book chronicling how Elon University used the literature on the conditions that enhance student development to inform an uncommonly wise strategic planning and institutional renewal effort to cultivate a student- and learning-centered culture characterized by challenging and innovative academic programs (Keller 2004). Today, Elon, with its 5,200 undergraduates spread across more than 50 majors, is about as close to a model of engaged learning as one can find.

Elon's institutional vision is both simple and powerful: to engage students' minds and inspire them to act as leaders and global citizens. The animating section of Elon's mission statement is a promise that the institution will live up to these four commitments:

- To nurture a rich intellectual community characterized by active student engagement with a faculty dedicated to excellent teaching and scholarly accomplishment.
- To provide a dynamic and challenging undergraduate curriculum grounded in the traditional liberal arts and sciences and complemented by distinctive professional and graduate programs.
- To integrate learning across the disciplines and put knowledge into practice, thus preparing students to be global citizens and informed leaders motivated by concern for the common good.
- To foster respect for human differences, passion for a life of learning, personal integrity, and an ethic of work and service.

At the core of Elon's effectiveness is its curricular model, which was overhauled in the early 1990s. The goal of the revision was to provide an educational experience that demanded that students delve deeper into the subjects they chose to study. To do so, the institution had to sacrifice breadth for depth. This was accomplished by reducing the standard student load from five three-credit courses an academic term to about four four-credit courses. An organizing principle for revising courses was that the additional credit hour had to be allocated to some form of experiential or inquiry-based learning—simply adding another class hour of lecture was not an acceptable approach. This, along with other curricular and cocurricular requirements and expectations, created both opportunities for more student participation in their education and a culture of engagement on the part of faculty and staff as well as students.

For example, Elon has 11 academic and student engagement centers devoted to such diverse topics and interests as entrepreneurial leadership, law and humanities, and ethnographic research and community studies. One of these centers is "Elon in Los Angeles," a nine-week summer experience for up to 40 students that combines several classes (acting, production, and public relations) and collaborative work on the culminating project—five short films that will eventually be screened at the American Film Institute. The films are produced and directed by students in the production class and feature students taking the acting class. The students in the public relations class assemble press kits containing plot synopses, cast lists, and production bios to circulate to attendees, and they craft a social media strategy for the films. Students also take part in film screenings, behind-the-scenes tours of productions in progress, and mentoring interactions with Elon graduates working and living in Los Angeles.

How engaged are Elon students in mission-relevant activities that were articulated as an institutional promise? Almost 66 percent of first-year students at least occasionally make class presentations, compared with only 35 percent of freshmen at other colleges and universities across the nation. Elon also is writing intensive, as 90 percent of freshmen and 80 percent of seniors write five or more five-page papers in a given academic year; another hefty percentage of freshmen (65 percent) wrote five or more papers of five to 19 pages. That is a lot of writing compared with the vast majority of colleges. Further, about one-third of Elon seniors take a service-learning course, which is about twice the national average. Finally, Elon seniors are much more likely than seniors across the nation to study abroad (79 percent), do an internship or field placement (92 percent), and have a culminating senior experience (94 percent).

These kinds of educational activities are available at almost every college or university. What makes Elon special along with other high-performing institutions is that they designate points in and outside the classroom where students cannot avoid these developmentally powerful experiences. Elon's efforts are reflected in its retention and graduation rates: first-year retention at Elon was 90 percent in 2010, and the six-year graduation rate was 81 percent, up from 69 percent in 2001 (Elon University 2012).

Other High-Impact Practices

All three of these institutions have intentionally focused on finding ways to ensure that most, if not all, of their students are exposed to one or more high-impact practices (HIPs). These practices—learning communities at Valencia; common intellectual experiences, such as Paideia, at Luther; and field experiences, such as "Elon in Los Angeles"—are called high-impact because undergraduate students who do them report much higher scores on NSSE engagement measures, such as academic challenge, active and collaborative learning, student-faculty interaction, and supportive campus environment, than peers who have not had similar experiences (Kuh 2008). This is because HIPs induce students to (among other things) invest substantial time and energy to educationally purposeful tasks, interact frequently with their teachers and peers, get feedback often, and apply what they are learning (Kuh 2008). In addition, students who have participated in at least one HIP report more frequent deep learning behaviors and benefit to a greater degree on various self-reported outcomes, such as personal-social development and practical competencies (Kuh 2008, 2010). A review of the literature lends additional support to these promising findings (Brownell and Swaner 2010) as do results from the ongoing Wabash National Study (Blaich 2009) and Pascarella and Terenzini's (2005) synthesis of research on college impact.

However, on many campuses, utilization of HIPs is unsystematic; many students may be left out of powerful learning experiences (Kuh 2008). When practices are designed for broad or almost universal student engagement, they help solidify the connection of students to their chosen college or university. And when these practices line up with the articulated values and goals of the institution, the distinctive brand or mission is strengthened and the promise to students is fulfilled.

Additional examples of high-impact practices include: first-year seminars and experiences, writing-intensive courses, collaborative assignments and projects, diversity/global learning, service learning or community-based learning, internships, undergraduate research, and capstone projects. These experiences make a tangible difference in student success. For example, "students who do research with faculty are more likely to persist, gain more intellectually and personally, and choose a research-related field as a career" (Kuh 2008, 14).

Two institutional examples of where high-impact learning practices have been implemented for a large proportion of students are the University of Michigan and Gonzaga University. For both of these institutions, first-year student retention is high—96 percent for the University of Michigan and 92 percent for Gonzaga; they also have impressive six-year graduation rates: 90 percent for the University of Michigan and 81 percent for Gonzaga (*U.S. News & World Report* 2011).

At the University of Michigan, "excellence" is the watchword for the intense, achievement-oriented campus culture. This large complex university dedicates considerable resources to the first-year experience, which includes the Undergraduate Research Opportunity Program (UROP). This campuswide program offers students the chance to engage in research with faculty, research scientists, and staff; about 1,100 students and 700 faculty participate each year (University of Michigan 2012). Many students participate in more than one UROP and find that the networking potential is powerful, leading to future academic and career success (Kuh et al. 2005).

At Gonzaga University in Spokane, Washington, the Jesuit model of educating the whole person—mind, body, and spirit—is animated in the strong institutional emphasis on service learning and civic engagement. As part of the core requirements in the College of Arts and Science, students must complete at least one course that includes a service-learning component—these courses aim to develop students' "thirst for justice" as promised in Gonzaga's mission. Gonzaga students also engage in service activities through the Honors Program Freshman Colloquium in which a 20-hour service component is linked to the academic program, as well as through the Center for Community Action and Service Learning that supports opportunities in which every component of a service project is planned and delivered by the students. Students report gaining practical experience in leadership, decision-making, and policymaking as well as forging meaningful relationships with peers, administrators, professors, and Spokane residents (Kuh et al. 2005).

As with other effective educational practices, the effects of participating in HIPs are positive for all types of students, but historically underserved students tend to benefit *more* from engaging in educationally purposeful activities than majority students in terms of first-year grade point average and first- to second-year retention (Kuh 2008). For example, at the University of Minnesota–Twin Cities, University of San Diego, and University of Georgia, the correlation between higher graduation rates and participating in the high-impact practice of study abroad is particularly strong for students of color and does not delay time to graduation (Redden 2012). The clear implication is that institutional leaders must ensure that enough of these opportunities are available to meet the demand and that they are implemented at a level of quality that will, indeed, deliver on the promise.

Lessons Learned

None of the institutions mentioned in this chapter are perfect. However, they have certain characteristics in common that make them instructive examples to consider.

First and foremost, the policies, programs, and practices to which students are exposed are enacted in ways congruent with the institution's espoused educational promise to students. Curricular requirements and cocurricular experiences are arranged and implemented in a way that demand that students reflect on, integrate, and apply their learning in systematic ways at multiple points during the baccalaureate experience. Active and collaborative learning and rigorous liberal arts educational approaches are the norm, such as writing-intensive courses and first-year seminars. Experiences with diversity inside and outside the classroom are valued. Students typically are required at different points in their studies to demonstrate what they have learned, including some form of a capstone class, portfolio, or project.

Aligning student expectations and experiences inside and outside the classroom with the institution's educational mission, brand promise, and curricular experiences is hard work. It requires time, focus, and considerable energy expended over an extended period of time. This cannot be done by setting policy or designing practice by anecdote or personal experience. Rather, reflecting and acting on systematically collected information about student and institutional performance are key, as this volume points out. Finally, another precious and essential ingredient to establishing a campus culture that fosters and supports student success is an ethic of "positive restlessness" (Kuh et al. 2005, 146)—a commitment to seek ways to deliver more of what we promise students.

At the end of the day, institutions that want to do better by their students can do so only by taking concrete steps toward that end. If the colleges and universities mentioned in this chapter and other high-performing schools can do it, so can many others.

References

Blaich, C. F. 2009, May/June. *High-Impact Practices and Experiences from the Wabash National Study.* Closing plenary address to the Association of American Colleges and Universities Institute on General Education and Assessment, Minneapolis.

Brownell, J. E., and L. E. Swaner. 2010. *Five High-Impact Practices: Research on Learning Outcomes, Completion, and Quality.* Washington, D.C.: Association of American Colleges and Universities.

Elon University. 2012. "Office of Insitutional Research—Common Data Sets: 2011–2012." Accessed June 28, 2012, http://www.elon.edu/e-web/administration/institutional _research/CDS/1112cds.xhtml.

Keller, G. 2004. *Transforming a College: The Story of a Little-Known College's Strategic Climb to National Distinction.* Baltimore: The Johns Hopkins University Press.

Kuh, G. D. 2007. "How to Help Students Achieve." *The Chronicle of Higher Education* 53(41):B12–13.

Kuh, G. D. 2008. *High-Impact Educational Practices: What They Are, Who Has Access to Them, and Why They Matter.* Washington, D.C.: Association of American Colleges and Universities.

Kuh, G. D. 2010. "Foreword: High-Impact Practices: Retrospective and Prospective." In *Five High-Impact Practices: Research on Learning Outcomes, Completion, and Quality,* edited by J. E. Brownell and L. E. Swaner, V–XIII. Washington, D.C.: Association of American Colleges and Universities.

Kuh, G. D., J. Kinzie, J. H. Schuh, E. J. Whitt, and Associates. 2005. *Student Success in College: Creating Conditions That Matter.* San Francisco: Jossey-Bass.

Luther College. 2012. "Mission Statement." Accessed August 14, 2012, http://www .luther.edu/about/mission/.

Pascarella, E. T., and P. T. Terenzini. 2005. *How College Affects Students: A Third Decade of Research,* vol. 2. San Francisco: Jossey-Bass.

Redden, E. 2012. "Study Abroad, Graduate on Time." Accessed August 1, 2012, http://www.insidehighered.com/news/2012/07/10/new-studies-link-study -abroad-time-graduation#ixzz22JxjAGXj.

University of Michigan. 2012. "Undergraduate Research Opportunity Program." Accessed August 14, 2012, http://www.lsa.umich.edu/urop/.

U.S. News & World Report. 2011. *Best Colleges 2012 Edition.* Washington, D.C.

Valencia Community College Planning Council. 2004. "Strategic Learning Plan Refresh Report." Accessed August 14, 2012, http://valenciacollege.edu/lci/documents /VCCrfrshSLPdec04.pdf.

GEORGE D. KUH *is an adjunct professor at the University of Illinois and chancellor's professor emeritus of higher education at Indiana University–Bloomington.*

NEW DIRECTIONS FOR HIGHER EDUCATION • DOI:10.1002/he

This chapter considers how addressing the essential role of faculty in an institution's retention efforts can be enhanced by leveraging new accreditation requirements regarding retention and graduation outcomes.

Engaging Faculty in Retention: Finding Traction through Accreditation

Caryn Chaden

Any institutional approach to improving graduation rates must include faculty. Faculty, more than anyone else, deliver an institution's *promise*, one course at a time. They also evaluate whether or not students have demonstrated sufficient mastery of the subject at hand to make *progress* toward their degrees. Indeed, as Vincent Tinto (2012, 114) writes in his most recent book, *Completing College: Rethinking Institutional Action*:

> For most institutions, especially those that are nonresidential, the classroom is the one place, perhaps the only place, where students meet each other and the faculty and engage in formal learning activities. For the great majority of students, success in college is most directly shaped by their experiences in the classroom.

Whether that classroom is a physical space or a virtual one, faculty's role in improving graduation rates by helping students succeed in coursework is critical.

In previous chapters of this volume, George Kuh and Charles Schroeder share examples of course-based practices that have been shown to contribute to students' engagement in their learning. Most often, *individual* faculty participate in such innovations and initiatives according to their interest rather than as part of an institution-wide approach to improving retention and graduation rates. Changing *institutional* expectations of faculty in order to improve retention and graduation rates is a far greater challenge. Yet in this era of accountability, institutions and their faculty may have no choice but to meet that challenge as their accreditation may now depend on it. And therein lies a powerful means for achieving institutional traction in its retention strategy that is so often missing.

NEW DIRECTIONS FOR HIGHER EDUCATION, no. 161, Spring 2013 © Wiley Periodicals, Inc.
Published online in Wiley Online Library (wileyonlinelibrary.com) • DOI:10.1002/he.20049

Why is Change So Hard?

At most institutions, faculty are rarely asked to think about their activities in light of institutional graduation rates. Traditionally, they have been hired to teach courses in their discipline, along with conducting research and service, and they have enjoyed the freedom to accomplish that task as they see fit. While many care deeply about the success of individual students, they typically have not been asked to consider what role they might play in improving institutional graduation rates, or what institutional impact coordinated efforts might have. Elevating the importance of degree completion among the priorities of faculty can be difficult for two reasons. First, the reward structure for tenured and tenure-track faculty typically emphasizes research as much as, if not more than, teaching. Second, many institutions rely increasingly on the work of adjunct faculty, who may teach isolated courses and have limited opportunity or incentive to engage in long-term, coordinated institutional efforts.

Elevating the importance of faculty engagement in retention-enhancing processes has institutional consequences and requires institutional commitments. For example, several of Kuh's recommended "high-impact practices" reviewed in chapter 8—first-year experience courses, intensive writing courses, internships, and capstone courses—assume relatively small class sizes. Deciding who should teach those courses is a faculty-resource challenge of the first order. And if some courses are targeted to have low enrollment caps to promote certain outcomes, then what can or should happen in the larger classes to promote a similar degree of involvement? What kind of institutional impact might result from widespread adoption of new practices? As just one small illustration, consider the seemingly simple recommendation that faculty provide students with ongoing feedback on a series of low-stakes assignments starting early in a course (Tinto 2012). To be sure, many faculty already engage in some version of this best practice, but many others do not, whether because of the numbers of students they teach, the number of responsibilities they juggle, the reward structure of their institution, or a simple lack of awareness of best practice in pedagogy. For instance, changing standard practice to incorporate more feedback to students could require one or more of the following (alone or in combination): rethinking syllabi and assignments, devoting additional time to providing feedback, assigning teaching assistants to provide the feedback, incorporating technology to provide the feedback, or shifting some attention away from research in a content area and toward a study of students' learning. Even if faculty wanted to embrace new practices, they might need institutional support to do so. Hence, while faculty are key players in any approach to improving retention and graduation rates, their combined individual efforts will not suffice alone; any significant improvement in retention and graduation rates will require an institutional commitment in areas such as hiring and promotion practices, faculty workload, use of technology, support services, and the like. And the larger the number and scope of possible changes, the more considerable the commitment required. Therein lies the greatest challenge. To date, the best hope for addressing that challenge nationwide comes from the external motivation provided by changes to accreditation requirements.

Accreditation in the United States: Evolving Criteria

In the United States, the Department of Education (DOE) holds colleges and universities accountable through institutional accreditation, carried out by six DOE-recognized independent regional agencies. Only these six accrediting agencies have the authority to deem American institutions of higher learning eligible for what now totals upward of $150 billion in federal financial aid each year. The agencies must meet certain "requirements for recognition," with those requirements broad enough to allow the agencies to carry them out in ways appropriate to their member institutions (U.S. Department of Education 2012).

Thus, the accrediting agencies serve a crucial role, explaining to institutions the criteria they must meet and holding them accountable to those criteria, while at the same time honoring the variety of missions and student profiles that has long been the hallmark of American higher education. Most importantly, with federal financial aid at stake, the accreditation process itself has become a lever for change, focusing the attention of administrators, faculty, and staff on aspects of institutional performance deemed important for all colleges and universities, no matter what the specific mission or population served.

Since the 2006 release of *A Test of Leadership: Charting the Future of U.S. Higher Education* (also known as "The Spellings Report"), which called for colleges and universities to demonstrate "improved accountability" for cost, price, and student success outcomes, accreditation agencies have responded by modifying accreditation standards to reflect the public's concerns (Spellings 2006). The most recent addition to accreditation standards focuses on retention and graduation rates.

While all six regional accrediting agencies now include language about retention and graduation, the newly revised Criteria for Accreditation recently approved by the Higher Learning Commission (HLC) of the North Central Association, which go into effect for reviews taking place starting in Fall 2012, are most instructive. Under the heading "Teaching and Learning: Evaluation and Improvement," the criteria include an entirely new "core component": "4.C. The institution demonstrates a commitment to educational improvement through ongoing attention to retention, persistence, and completion rates in its degree and certificate programs" (Higher Learning Commission 2012). All institutions accredited by the HLC must demonstrate that they meet this core component. Under it, the document includes sub-components that the Commission "seeks to ensure are not overlooked." These include the following:

1. The institution has defined goals for student retention, persistence, and completion that are ambitious but attainable and appropriate to its mission, student population, and educational offerings.
2. The institution collects and analyzes information on student retention, persistence, and completion of its programs.
3. The institution uses information on student retention, persistence, and completion of programs to make improvements as warranted by the data.
4. The institution's processes and methodologies for collecting and analyzing information on student retention, persistence, and completion of programs reflect good practice.

Per federal reporting requirements, institutions have long collected data on student retention, persistence, and completion and submitted them to the Integrated Postsecondary Education Data System (IPEDS). But reporting a standard set of data is no longer sufficient; institutions must now *demonstrate* the ways in which they analyze and act on this data to improve their programs. These new criteria for accreditation call on institutions to move discussions of retention and completion from the margins of institutional effort and engage in a much broader discussion with faculty and other stakeholders of what constitutes "educational improvement" given their individual mission and student profile, what processes need to be in place to facilitate improvement, and how students' progress is to be measured. In effect, it calls for a 4 Ps perspective on student retention.

Potential Lever for Change

Since the federal reporting requirements produce a common data set nationwide, tools for collecting, analyzing, and even comparing data are already in place to support these conversations about retention and graduation rates. For example, The Education Trust's (2012) "College Results Online" website uses IPEDS data "to provide policymakers, counselors, parents, students, and others with information about college graduation rates" for four-year institutions or groups of students. However, using data to improve retention and degree completion requires another level of institutional involvement altogether. Staff professionals who provide various kinds of support have long been closest to this issue, working with students to orient them to the institution, advise them on their academic programs, recommend potential internship or career opportunities, tutor them in subjects like math and writing, encourage them to participate in cocurricular activities, and help them stay on track for graduation. From a 4 Ps perspective, these staff professionals contribute to students' *progress* by charting the way and helping to remove barriers to success, while also helping to fulfill the institution's *promise* by pointing students to enriching activities within and beyond the curriculum.

Yet as crucial as these efforts are, they can only go so far. If the primary site of students' formal learning is their coursework, then any efforts to improve institutional rates of retention and graduation will require faculty to engage in reflecting on the experiences they create for their students. Already, as Kuh discusses in chapter 8, "high-impact practices" have been shown to increase students' engagement with their own learning. However, the relationship between students' learning and timely degree completion is not yet clear. We know from Tinto and others that "the more students are academically and socially engaged with other people on campus, especially with faculty and student peers, the more likely (other things being equal) they will stay and graduate from college" (Tinto 2012, 64; Astin 1993; Greene 2005; Kuh et al. 2005). However, as Richard Arum and Josipa Roksa argue in *Academically Adrift: Limited Learning on College Campuses* (2011), enhanced relationships do not necessarily lead to enhanced learning. It makes intuitive sense that students who are engaged in their own learning would also tend to complete their degrees in a timely way, but more research is needed to test that hypothesis.

In light of the new accreditation requirements, national discussions of retention and degree completion promise to gain a new level of support and sophistication, with more research focused not only on determining which practices are associated with increases in students' engagement in learning, but on which practices—both within and outside formal coursework—are associated with students staying in school and completing their degrees. Such data will help guide institutions and their faculty toward adopting practices that will make a difference. While this prospect may appear overly optimistic, there is precedent for accreditation criteria being a lever for positive institutional change, most notably in the assessment of students' learning.

Assessment of Students' Learning: From Compliance to Commitment

The evolution of assessment of students' learning provides a window into what may result from the inclusion of a focus on retention and graduation rates in accreditation criterion. The initial development of assessment as a field has been well documented (Ewell 2002), but the role of accreditation standards in bringing along initially reluctant institutions continues to be noteworthy. While each of the regional accrediting agencies uses somewhat different language in their criteria, each of them requires institutions of higher learning to demonstrate that they have articulated learning goals for each of their programs, that they assess the degree to which students are accomplishing those goals, and that they use the information they glean from these assessments to improve their programs. From a 4 Ps perspective, learning is essential to an institution's *promise*, but assessment of student learning is a *process* issue. Who actually performs the tasks associated with assessment? What steps does the process require? What materials do the person or persons performing the assessment review?

In the late '80s and '90s, when criteria for accreditation first began requiring institutions to demonstrate how they were assessing student learning, many institutions simply did not know how to answer these questions or what to do beyond what faculty had always done: build curricula based on pertinent topics and material to be covered and assign grades based on an evaluation of individual students' work in individual classes. Yet evaluating an individual student's work in any given class is a very different task from evaluating a student group's mastery of a set of learning outcomes that cuts across multiple courses in a major, or, as with general education learning outcomes, cuts across multiple degree programs.

To address these complexities, an institution's first impulse may be to circumvent faculty altogether and adopt one of the myriad centrally administered assessment tools spawned by the accreditation criterion. However, these tools, from indirect assessment measures like the widely used National Survey of Student Engagement (NSSE) to direct measures like the Collegiate Learning Assessment (CLA), all have serious limitations in terms of evaluating what students actually learn in college (Harris, Smith, and Harris 2011; Soares 2012). The CLA website itself includes a link to a cautionary statement from the influential Council for Aid to Education Board of Trustees reaffirming the board's commitment to "helping American colleges and universities measure and improve learning outcomes for their students," but emphasizing that the CLA is only one of many tools supporting assessment (Council for Aid to Education n.d., 1). Experts now agree that any meaningful assessment of students' learning necessarily includes some direct assessment of the work they produce in classes across the curriculum for a particular program.

Of course, thoughtful curriculum-based assessment is labor-intensive—it involves a coordinated set of specific activities: agreeing on program learning outcomes, mapping those outcomes onto courses, creating rubrics for evaluation, collecting samples of work, evaluating the work, analyzing the data, recommending any necessary changes to the curriculum, and then going through the process again over time to see if the changes made any difference. And, as we have seen, shifting the institutional culture to accommodate the time and effort required for these activities is itself a challenge. No wonder, then, that a common topic for follow-up requirements in accreditation reviews concerns criteria related to the assessment of student learning. For example, an analysis of required follow-up reports for the HLC revealed that between 2008 and 2011, "assessment" was the most common topic for these reports, accounting for 24 percent of them; "finances" were next, accounting for 17 percent (Delaney 2012).

Recognizing this challenge, the Association of American Colleges and Universities (AAC&U), the National Institute for Learning Outcomes Assessment (NILOA) and the accrediting agencies themselves, often in conversation, have created an increasingly sophisticated infrastructure to support faculty, staff, and administrators in best practices, including an array of workshops, institutes, and online resources. In particular, AAC&U's "Liberal Education and America's Promise" (LEAP) initiative, launched in 2005, provides "essential learning outcomes" for the 21st century, and faculty and assessment experts from across the country are working together through the VALUE project (Valid Assessment of Learning in Undergraduate Education) to create rubrics for evaluating those learning outcomes (Association of American Colleges and Universities 2012). Since 2008, NILOA has helped institutions "discover and disseminate ways that academic programs and institutions can productively use assessment data internally to inform and strengthen undergraduate education, and externally to communicate with policy makers, families, and other stakeholders" (National Institute for Learning Outcomes Assessment 2012, para. 1).

With the support of these groups, institutions around the country have responded to the accreditation requirements by clarifying learning goals, coordinating assessment efforts, and introducing more "high-impact practices." If the numbers and range of related topics of sessions at annual meetings of the AAC&U and the accreditation agencies—not to mention specific conferences focused on assessment and on practices like e-portfolios—are any indication, colleges and universities across the country are taking the assessment of students' learning seriously. Faculty, often in cooperation with chairs and associate deans, are working to formulate meaningful questions and using what they discover to help their students learn more. At many institutions, what began as reluctant compliance has become genuine commitment to the process of using assessment of students' learning to improve academic programs.

Lessons Learned

The story of the evolution of learning assessment provides some important lessons for mobilizing an institutional retention strategy. First, a targeted external requirement, thoughtfully and flexibly implemented, can provide a strong impetus for change in both institutional behavior and the national conversation about such basic features of higher education as learning and degree completion. Second, institutions need support and instruction from the accrediting bodies themselves, in cooperation with pertinent professional organizations, in order to fully understand the expectation, the reasons behind it, and best practices in carrying it out. Only then will institutions be able to determine how best to proceed. Third, if the requirement truly makes good sense as faculty and staff learn more over time, at least some of them will become genuinely interested and engaged by the intellectual inquiry itself. How *do* we best assess what students have learned? What *does* it take for a student to succeed and learn what they need to learn? These are complex questions with complex answers—exactly what higher education is all about.

The final lesson to be learned from the example of assessment is that there are no easy answers. The more focused assessment efforts have become in various disciplines, the clearer it is that no single instrument can answer the question: "What have students learned?"

Next Steps: Research and Changing Practices

Now that accreditation criteria also include a focus on retention and graduation rates, the conversation about these issues on the national and institutional level promises to evolve over time and institutional practice will improve and expand as well. In particular, since so much work has already been done to identify "high-impact practices" for learning, the next logical step is to look more closely at the relationship between such practices and degree completion. And while "high-impact practices" can happen across the curriculum, there is the need for more research into more discipline-specific practices that both encourage students' learning and contribute to their successfully completing their majors and their degrees. Finally, there is need for more research into practices that can be scaled for use in large classes and large institutions. Some of the best work on scaling best practices to large institutions has been done by Carol Twigg and the National Center for Academic Transformation (2001); the Center's website includes reports on early research linking these practices to moderate increases in degree completion for targeted populations.

At a minimum, the new accreditation criteria will require institutions to explicitly address issues of retention and degree completion or face the prospect of even greater scrutiny from their accrediting agency. If the experience with the assessment of student learning is any indication, the road forward will not be smooth; it will likely involve a good number of follow-up reports required of institutions that, at least initially, do not demonstrate they have fully met the criteria. In order to redress those gaps, many institutions will adopt new processes and practices designed to help increase retention and graduation rates. The more everyone understands that retention and degree completion are the concerns of the entire institution and the more invested faculty become in addressing this challenge, the more likely it is that institutions will then need to align faculty hiring practices, reward structures, and allocations of resources with this new priority. What works well for one institution may be less appropriate for others, depending on the student profile and institutional mission. However, if faculty engagement is as critical to retention strategy at the institutional level as the theory and research says it is, using the accreditation process to achieve that engagement is a powerful lever for change. As part of that process, a 4 Ps framework can help institutions sort out the various factors contributing to retention and degree completion rates and consider how these factors might be aligned to meet institutional goals. And if the story of assessment is any guide, the new accreditation criteria focused on improving retention and graduation rates will lead, over time, to more genuine commitment to a central *promise* of higher education.

References

Arum, R., and J. Roksa. 2011. *Academically Adrift: Limited Learning on College Campuses*. Chicago: The University of Chicago Press.

Association of American Colleges and Universities. 2012. "Liberal Education and America's Promise (LEAP) – Essential Learning Outcomes." Accessed August 22, 2012, http://www.aacu.org/leap/vision.cfm.

Astin, A. 1993. *What Matters in College? Four Critical Years Revisited*. San Francisco: Jossey Bass.

Council for Aid to Education (CAE). n.d. "Council for Aid to Education (CAE) Board of Trustees Statement on the Role of Assessment in Higher Education." Accessed August 23, 2012, http://www2.ed.gov/about/bdscomm/list/hiedfuture/4th-meeting/benjamin.pdf.

Delaney, K. 2012, March. "Overview of the Commission's Monitoring through Reports: When, How, and Whether Monitoring has an Impact on Quality." Paper presented at the annual meeting of the Higher Learning Commission, Chicago.

Ewell, P. T. 2002. "An Emerging Scholarship: A Brief History of Assessment." In *Building a Scholarship of Assessment*, edited by T. W. Banta and Associates, 3–25. San Francisco: Jossey-Bass.

Greene, T. 2005. "Bridging the Divide: Exploring the Relationship Between Student Engagement and Educational Outcomes for African American and Hispanic Community College Students in the State of Florida." PhD diss., University of Texas at Austin.

Harris, P., B. Smith, and J. Harris. 2011. *The Myths of Standardized Tests: Why They Don't Tell You What You Think They Do*. Lanham, Md.: Rowman & Littlefield Publishers, Inc.

Higher Learning Commission. 2012. "The New Criteria for Accreditation." Accessed August 23, 2012, http://ncahlc.org/Information-for-Institutions/criteria-and-core-components.html.

Kuh, G. D., J. Kinzie, J. H. Schuh, E. J. Whitt, and Associates. 2005. *Student Success in College: Creating Conditions That Matter*. San Francisco: Jossey-Bass.

National Center for Academic Transformation. 2001. Accessed August 22, 2012, www.thencat.org.

National Institute for Learning Outcomes Assessment. 2012. "Our Mission & Vision." Accessed August 22, 2012, http://www.learningoutcomeassessment.org/AboutUs.html.

Soares, J. A. 2012. *SAT Wars: The Case for Test-Optional Admissions*. New York: Teachers College Press, Columbia University.

Spellings, M. 2006. *A Test of Leadership: Charting the Future of U.S. Higher Education*. Washington D.C.: U.S. Department of Education.

The Education Trust. 2012. "College Results Online." Accessed August 23, 2012, http://www.collegeresults.org/.

Tinto, V. 2012. *Completing College: Rethinking Institutional Action*. Chicago: The University of Chicago Press.

U.S. Department of Education. 2012. "Boards & Commissions – Accreditation in the United States – Subpart B – The Criteria For Recognition – Basic Eligibility Requirements." Accessed August 22, 2012, http://www2.ed.gov/admins/finaid/accred/accreditation_pg13 .html#RecognitionCriteria.

CARYN CHADEN *is an associate vice president for Academic Affairs and associate professor of English at DePaul University.*

10

This chapter summarizes some of the themes that characterize a 4 Ps orientation to institutional retention strategy and offers an example of how one institution has used this approach to structure its retention efforts.

The 4 Ps as a Guiding Perspective

David H. Kalsbeek

A 4 Ps perspective addresses immediate needs: to help institutions gain traction in their retention strategies by framing and reframing the challenges and the possible responses, by challenging some of the traditional mental models about retention that can distract or dilute those strategies, and by offering focus and coherence to institutional efforts. In conclusion, there is merit in identifying some of the key themes that emerge throughout the essays in this volume, discussing the implications for how institutions can organize their retention efforts, and outlining some ways a 4 Ps framework can be used at the institutional level.

Key Themes of a 4 Ps Framework

Retention Strategy Begins with Institutional Self-Awareness. Retention strategies need to speak to the circumstances and contexts of specific institutions. In other words, all retention is local. Yet at the same time, as argued in chapter 2, institutions operate within a larger higher education environment that is characterized by patterns and symmetries conditioned by the marketplace. The work of defining and building a successful retention strategy needs to be grounded in a shared understanding of the limits and opportunities imposed by this environment and the institution's position within it.

Without an honest self-appraisal of the institution's market profile and an acknowledgment of how that dictates its retention and completion rates in predictable ways, retention goals lack the necessary moorings for meaningful planning. For example, most institutions want to know how their retention performance compares with their peers. However, unless those peer institutions exhibit broadly similar market profiles, the comparisons are likely to be of little relevance.

NEW DIRECTIONS FOR HIGHER EDUCATION, no. 161, Spring 2013 © Wiley Periodicals, Inc.
Published online in Wiley Online Library (wileyonlinelibrary.com) • DOI:10.1002/he.20050

Retention Strategy Requires Addressing Structural Conditions for Institutional Improvement. The retention literature is replete with calls for shaping the cultural conditions for improving retention, assuming that the obstacles to improvement rest in deeply seated institutional values. Calls for creating an institutional culture focused on retention must compete with the simultaneous calls on campus for creating a culture of assessment, a culture of philanthropy, a culture of compliance, a culture of excellence, a culture of tolerance, and so on. While retention advocates argue for a focus on culture to address the deepest of institutional values and the most fundamental of all possible changes, perhaps that focus is why nothing seems to improve.

At the opposite extreme, the retention literature is also replete with interventionist approaches, reflected best in Seidman's retention formula (2012), which is perhaps the quintessential expression of an interventionist orientation to retention. Certainly, creating practices and programs as interventions can successfully assist some populations of students to better navigate academic and institutional conditions that otherwise would hamper student success, but interventions, by definition, are accommodations to the prevailing and often problematic structures of academic institutions. They accept the prevailing conditions as givens, help students work around them, and thereby risk missing opportunities for real institutional change.

Rather than either cultural or interventionist approaches, a 4 Ps framework turns attention to the structures themselves: administrative policies, the academic calendar, course design, and curricular pathways that are of our deliberate creation and typically reflect today's solutions to yesterday's problems. By focusing on specific institutional policies and practices and creating "structures of opportunity" at the intersections of student behavior and institutional arrangements, a 4 Ps framework gains traction for improvement by avoiding both the vagaries of culture change and the reactive work-arounds of interventionism.

Improvement Requires Connecting Retention Efforts to Core Institutional Activities. One of the more common complaints by retention advocates is the difficulty of pushing retention onto the already crowded agenda for institutional attention at the highest level. Rather than trying to elevate retention as one additional and independent strategic initiative, a 4 Ps framework focuses instead on strengthening the interconnections of retention strategy with other broad institutional goals, activities, and outcomes. As seen in chapter 9, as an explicit component of accreditation review, retention becomes an integral part of the ongoing focus on teaching and learning and the institution's development of faculty roles and activities rather than one more piled-on expectation or the concern of a few well-intentioned professors. Another approach is to use an institution's brand identity and brand promise to prioritize improvements in the student experience thereby connecting retention with the core institutional marketing strategy. We do not normally think of student services or cocurricular activities in the context of an institution's brand. And yet, as argued in chapter 5, they may have a great deal to do with how an institution lives out its brand promise. A 4 Ps perspective can help inform an institutional dialogue that illuminates the connections between how the institution is viewed in the marketplace and the actual experiences it provides. It clarifies what the institution needs to do to live up to (and go beyond) the expectations students have for it. These examples reflect an approach to retention that seeks not to compete with other institutional activities and priorities but to connect with them; this is accomplished through cross-functional dialogue that fosters administrative and academic integration.

Measuring the Quality of Persistence is What Matters Most. For educators, the temptation is great to take retention and cast it in terms of student learning, student success, and student engagement. While these are essential and far-reaching educational goals and outcomes, the risk is that they can so obfuscate the direct goal of improving rates of degree completion that either nothing gets off the ground or retention strategies deviate to attend to things that may correlate with retention but don't directly impact it. It is hard to build traction toward nebulous and often immeasurable outcomes, however important those outcomes may be. Working toward quantifiably measurable goals is a requisite ingredient for gaining ground in improving institutional degree completion rates.

By that standard, a singular focus on persistence also fails, since persistence does not necessarily equate to progress toward degree completion. Persistence is more easily and precisely measureable than learning outcomes, more easily comparable across different disciplines or populations or institutions, and perhaps even easier to improve than completion rates. However, it falls short as an institutional goal because cohort persistence rates look backward. They are by definition measured against a starting point in time, not progress toward a future outcome.

It is the quality of student persistence—the measurable advancement toward degree completion—that matters most and is often masked by prevailing attention to persistence alone (Kalsbeek 2008). Developing a diligent and vigilant focus on metrics that track students' progress toward the specific, defined goal of degree completion is a necessary ingredient for traction in institutional retention strategy. If improving graduation rates is an institutional aspiration, then the quality of student progress toward that goal must be as clearly defined, as transparent, and as well communicated to all stakeholders as first- to second-year persistence metrics generally are.

Institutional Improvement Requires Bringing Innovation to Scale. One of the attractive things about student retention is that improving it is generally considered a worthy goal by all; as a result, nearly every initiative or project can argue that its impact on student retention justifies some added resource allocation. An all-too-common petition is that "if we retain only one more student through this new initiative, it will pay for itself"; sum all such requests campuswide and it's likely that a college must retain

110% of its freshman class to recoup the accumulated promises of return on investment.

Moving a broad institutional metric like the overall graduation rate typically requires more comprehensive innovation, real structural change, and bringing to scale some of the practices and approaches that often are proven to work at smaller institutions or with smaller populations. A 4 Ps focus on broad-based process improvement or on delivering the brand promise for every student is an effective strategy for pushing retention strategy to the scale and scope necessary for real institutional gains.

An essential element in bringing innovation to scale is technology, and ongoing improvements in campus technologies and data systems are a necessary part of retention strategy. Many so-called retention systems are simply applications of customer relationship management (CRM) technologies that enhance targeted and individualized communications with students. However, the technological innovations most required for improving rates of degree completion aren't only those that enhance communications with students, but rather those that directly remove barriers to students' progress toward degree.

For example, online degree audit and degree-progress reporting systems provide students, advisors, and faculty a necessary roadmap toward timely degree completion. More importantly, the process of developing and implementing such systems inevitably surfaces many of the curricular obstacles and impediments to students' degree progress. They enable the discovery of the ways by which students actually work their way through the curriculum, which often is quite different from what faculty have designed.

Another example is classroom and course scheduling systems that not only improve institutional use of its facilities and faculty resources but also can identify bottlenecks and limitations in course offerings that hamper timely degree progress. These systems are often implemented for operational efficiencies in classroom assignments, but if they are embraced as part of a retention strategy, they provide rich insight about how the institution's patterns of course offerings may be insufficiently attuned to student course requirements and, by extension, affordability considerations.

Improving Retention Requires Balancing Tensions and Tradeoffs. As with most institutional decisions and commitments, a focus on retention implies less attention or resources dedicated to other objectives—tradeoffs are givens in a context of scarce and shrinking resources. At a deeper level, improving retention creates real tensions with other goals because of the interdependencies and intercorrelations of retention with other enrollment outcomes. A 4 Ps framework does not eliminate these tensions but can clarify them, thereby facilitating institutional choices and priority setting. In a 4 Ps scheme, not all objectives are created equal; some rise to the top as the institution defines its profile and promise. Some retention initiatives provide for a much higher level of integration and complementarity than others, thereby affecting a plurality of students in powerful ways.

NEW DIRECTIONS FOR HIGHER EDUCATION • DOI:10.1002/he

A 4 Ps framework embraces the inherent tensions and tradeoffs in any retention strategy and deliberately works to place retention goals in that context. For example, when academic progress is elevated as an outcome, it may be at the expense of deep learning. When processes are automated and transactions shift online, students may lose the opportunity for one-on-one contact with faculty and staff who can advise and mentor them. And, when students of a particular profile are targeted for enrollment because they likely will have better retention and graduation outcomes, this may conflict with the historic mission or public charter of the institution to provide access to other populations of students.

There is an overused aphorism that "retention is more cost-effective than recruitment," suggesting that it is unquestionably more economical to retain an enrolled student than to recruit a new one. The reality, though, is usually far more complex because improving retention generally introduces other costs and tradeoffs. A 4 Ps perspective recognizes that every enrollment goal exists in tension with others and that improving institutional outcomes like retention in all likelihood requires balancing strategic tradeoffs with diversity, access, quality, net revenue, etc. The framework encourages institutional leadership to ask how retention goals and strategy intersect with all of the other strategies designed to shape the desired enrollment profile and how they can be effectively and simultaneously balanced as part of the institution's multifaceted enrollment, academic, financial, and strategic plans and priorities.

How to Organize for Retention

One of the more widely debated issues in the retention literature is how to organize for an effective institutional retention strategy.

On the one hand, simply repeating the old bromide that "retention is everyone's responsibility" is a sure path to inaction. While everyone can have a positive impact on any student's experience, the actual responsibility for improving institutional retention outcomes can never rest equally with every member of the faculty and staff. Everyone at the institution also can and does have an impact on new student recruitment, but the actual responsibility for orchestrating the institutional marketing and recruitment strategy nevertheless rests somewhere and with someone.

At the other extreme is the concept of the so-called "retention czar," a position with responsibility for retention programs, policies, and practices; from a 4 Ps perspective, this approach is likely just as problematic. While recent studies (College Board 2011) have defined such positions as indicative of a serious institutional commitment to retention, they can also signal a marginalization of that effort by confining the retention strategy to something so narrowly defined that it can actually be overseen by a single position with singular responsibility for retention. Arguing that a retention strategy requires an institution to have one retention office or officer responsible only for retention outcomes and having policy and budgetary authority to effect change is not likely a realistic or workable alternative.

There are certainly examples of institutions that have directors of retention who successfully function in an expanded ombudsman role and with an interventionist orientation. There are retention directors overseeing various student support services integrated administratively to help improve student academic success and retention. But when one frames an institution's retention strategy with a 4 Ps framework, several realizations immediately come into sharp relief.

First, if retention and completion rates improve when retention strategies connect to and leverage core structures and institutional processes, then elevating and specifying retention outcomes as an explicit responsibility of senior officers who can directly shape institutional policies, practices, and processes is likely to have far more impact than delegating that responsibility to an independent, retention-focused administrative role. For example, having retention outcomes identified explicitly as one of the top five areas of accountability for the chief enrollment officer is likely to be far more impactful than having a mid-level staff position dedicated 100 percent to retention because that senior-level officer already has oversight and responsibility for many of the core processes and structures shaping enrollment outcomes. Explicitly making retention rates as important an outcome for the enrollment management effort as admit rates, discount rates, diversity, and quality measures will likely have far greater impact than having a single retention office at the margin of institutional activity.

Second, retention committees can, in fact, also effectively lead institutional strategy, but only if chaired by or comprised of senior-level academic and administrative officers who have both the capacity to shape policies, practices, expectations, and processes and the responsibility to do so. The reality is that few institutions have additional resources to put toward retention strategies, so reallocations and reprioritizations are the order of the day. Finding ways of leveraging resources through cross-functional structures in academic, cocurricular, and administrative areas via collaborative processes and programs and deliberately tying retention strategies to ongoing core activities require the engagement of senior-level leadership in retention committees.

Third, since effective institutional action requires support and coordination, the locus for that focus matters. The decision about centering the responsibility for coordinating retention efforts in student affairs, academic affairs, or enrollment management is not inconsequential, and each option brings its own set of advantages and disadvantages (Kalsbeek 2007). It is a choice that often determines in real ways how the retention challenge will be formulated and framed since each organizational alignment approaches the retention effort with the distinct paradigms unique to that professional perspective.

The bias in a 4 Ps framework is toward anchoring retention in an active and equal collaboration between enrollment management and academic affairs. First, an enrollment management approach ensures that retention and completion rates are framed as institutional enrollment metrics inseparable from the institution's other enrollment goals; it also ensures that retention strategy benefits from the data-rich, goal-oriented, and broad-based orientation that is characteristic of enrollment management strategies. But retention strategies can only gain traction if they connect with core academic structures and processes. Senior academic leadership and engagement are required to ensure that retention strategies work effectively across academic units, that the faculty roles in those strategies are incorporated into broader expectations for faculty work, and that curricular structures and academic policies and processes are all on the agenda for improvement.

Other models can and do work; the key is being aware of how organizational placement can dictate the manner by which the retention agenda will be framed.

How to Use a 4 Ps Framework

This volume began by affirming the power of mental models in the ways organizations work. They are the assumptions that frame the ways we view challenges and define problems, what information is considered relevant, and the range of possible solutions envisioned. A 4 Ps framework attempts to make these assumptions about retention explicit, to challenge prevailing perspectives that may hamper institutional improvement, and to provide a clarifying focus on those elements that matter most in gaining institutional traction. The 4 Ps primarily provide heuristic value as a simple rubric for focusing on opportunities for real institutional improvement.

The first use of the 4 Ps is to guide the retention research agenda and expand it beyond the longitudinal cohort tracking models of persistence and the statistical analyses of "at risk" student populations that characterize much retention research. A 4 Ps–oriented retention research agenda also includes:

- Market research about an institution's market profile and its brand;
- Admission research on how non-traditional admission criteria or programs can more effectively shape a student profile favoring retention outcomes;
- Econometric analysis of how alternative tuition pricing and financial aid packaging regimens can be leveraged to affect not only new student yield and net revenue outcomes but also longer-term retention and degree completion;
- Comprehensive assessments of the student experience that gauge the degree to which students are engaged in high-impact educational opportunities consistent with the institution's brand and mission;

- Assessments of the extent to which faculty use course-based practices promoting progress, such as providing early feedback on student performance, use of Supplemental Instruction, etc.; and
- Curricular analyses of student pathways toward degree completion that identify the roadblocks, bottlenecks, and capacity limitations to academic progress.

Second, a 4 Ps framework is useful in the necessary task of educating campus communities about the importance of retention efforts and outcomes. The principles and perspectives of a 4 Ps framework can help key constituencies, such as deans, faculties, trustees, and student affairs professionals, move beyond typical and traditional assumptions of interventionist models. It highlights and clarifies for such audiences the importance of institutional profile, of moving from persistence to progress metrics, of addressing broad processes that improve outcomes for the many rather than only focusing on needs of the few, and of the need to create a campus experience that solidifies the institution's position, brand, and mission. Most importantly, it provides a simple structure and coherence to the institutional dialogue about what matters most in campus retention strategies.

Likewise, a 4 Ps framework is useful in the work of committees and officers charged with the oversight of retention initiatives, strategies, and outcomes. First, in addition to framing the research and analysis agenda, the 4 Ps assist in setting institutional goals and objectives informed by the entire context of institutional market position and enrollment dynamics. Second, in pursuit of those institutional goals, a 4 Ps framework offers a rubric for categorizing, mapping, and prioritizing the extraordinary breadth of activities that can and do shape profile, progress, process, and promise outcomes and conveys that the discrete pieces in this framework add up to more than the sum of the parts.

The 4 Ps can bring coherence and structure to an otherwise daunting retention agenda. As a framework for thinking about strategies for improving institutional retention and completion rates, the 4 Ps can provide a valuable focus institutions may require for building awareness of the dynamics shaping retention, for prioritizing institutional initiatives, for gaining traction in implementing strategies, and for making progress toward these important goals.

Moving Forward with a 4 Ps Framework

Tables 10.1–4 offer one example of how the 4 Ps have helped structure the institutional retention agenda at DePaul University. The 4 Ps were developed at DePaul as a guiding framework for institutional retention planning, evaluation, and improvement. These sample tables illustrate ways that the leaders of DePaul's Executive Retention Group have enhanced the

Table 10.1. Key Assumptions of DePaul University's Student Retention Strategy

Profile	Progress	Process	Promise
An institution's retention and graduation rates are bounded by the institution's profile and market position, making them highly predictable and more a function of what the institution is rather than what it does.	If the goal of an institutional retention strategy is degree attainment, then a focus on persistence (which is currently the norm) is perhaps the least desirable of all outcomes if it doesn't entail progress toward degree completion.	While there are student characteristics that are related to greater or lesser likelihood of degree completion, a strategic institutional response gives priority attention to processes and policies that either help or hinder all students' continuous enrollment.	Students enroll at institutions with expectations and aspirations that the institution will live up to its specific "brand promise"—that their experiences will be congruent with what the institution's mission and brand identity promise they will be.
These realities must shape how the institution sets its retention goals. Likewise, retention and graduation rates of specific student populations must be evaluated in an appropriate comparative context.	What is consistently the most significant predictor of likelihood to graduate is academic progress in the first quarter and first year—both grades and credits earned—since those are the metrics that reflect early progress toward degree.	At large, complex institutions, there are ample opportunities for improving student retention by focusing on integrating and streamlining the core enrollment processes related to admission, housing, advising, registration, billing, and financial aid.	Improved retention is the natural outcome of realizing the broader goal of ensuring congruence between student expectations and the reality of each student's entire educational experience in and out of the classroom. Ensuring that the student experience is consistent with how the market sees the value of the institution's brand not only improves retention but also reinforces the institution's brand.
Retention strategies are inextricably interrelated with admission strategies and must therefore be developed in a way fully integrated and balanced with the rest of DePaul's enrollment management goals (i.e., quality, diversity, access, affordability, net tuition revenue, and student mix) since all of these goals exist in tension one with another.	Ensuring that students make satisfactory academic progress toward degree completion over their years of college enrollment must be the primary focus of any retention effort.	Retention strategies should focus on the quality of all students' encounters with the processes, programs, policies, and personnel that compose the overall institutional environment.	

Table 10.2. Key Questions Guiding DePaul University's Student Retention Strategy

Profile	Progress	Process	Promise
How do we establish appropriate goals for institutional retention and graduation rates that align with the balance of DePaul's academic, student, and financial profile?	How do we ensure that students make timely, continuous, and satisfactory progress toward degree completion?	How do we integrate business processes and student services to create a seamless and supportive experience for students as they register for courses, manage their financial arrangements, and navigate DePaul toward degree completion?	How do we ensure that students' experiences meet or exceed their expectations for a DePaul education? (According to DePaul's brand research, these expectations are: academic challenge and engagement; a practical, values-based orientation; a campus environment that embraces diversity in all its forms; active immersion in the urban realities of Chicago; and highly responsive student services.)
How can we develop and implement admission practices, policies, and strategies that enable us to simultaneously identify and admit students who will succeed at DePaul, fulfill a mission of access, and elevate DePaul's academic profile?	How do we help students have a successful transition into college and experience early academic success?	How can we make best use of online tools and technologies to improve processes that support students' progress toward reaching their goals?	How do we ensure that all students have the opportunity to experience the full benefits of this brand promise?
How can we focus enrollment, pricing, and financial aid strategies in ways that reduce the financial barriers to degree completion?	How do we help students identify their educational goals; be purposeful in their approach to their education; and integrate the academic, career, and financial dimensions of their educational planning and progress toward degree attainment?	How do we configure and reconfigure physical space and staffing structures at DePaul to optimize the integration of academic, advising, and enrollment support services?	
How can we improve overall institutional rates of retention and degree completion while simultaneously expanding access and increasing diversity, knowing those goals are in tension with retention rates?	How can we identify the structural impediments to timely degree progress, such as curricular obstacles, inadequate course offerings, "killer courses" with high failure rates, inadequate math placement policies, and so on?	How do we ensure that students' encounters with the institution contribute to their satisfaction with university services?	

Table 10.3. Key High-Priority Goals and Selected Implemented Initiatives of DePaul University's Student Retention Strategy

Profile	Progress	Process	Promise
Goal: Elevate the academic profile of entering student classes while keeping a mission-balanced financial and demographic mix.	*Goal: Ensure students' initial academic success and continuous academic progress toward a DePaul degree.*	*Goal: Improve and integrate all processes and services related to students' enrollment at DePaul.*	*Goal: Ensure all students' expectations and experiences are consistent with the promise of DePaul's mission and brand.*
Create new curricula (e.g., health sciences major) to increase demand and strengthen student and market profile.	Create a First-Year Academic Success program offering prerequisite math and writing courses during the summer for no tuition or credit.	Create DePaul Central, a one-stop service center for Student Records, Financial Aid, and Student Accounts transactions, including walk-in, online, and phone service integration.	Expand and enhance the Chicago Quarter program to engage freshmen in a Chicago-immersion course in the first quarter.
Expand transfer enrollment to alleviate pressure on freshman enrollment growth goals.	Redesign specified "gateway" courses in math, chemistry, and accounting to reduce drop/fail/withdraw (DFW) rates.	Create Learning Center to better integrate tutoring and academic support services such as Writing Labs and Math Labs.	Create the Junior Year Experiential Learning requirement within the general education program where all undergraduates must participate in internships, study abroad, service learning courses, or independent research projects.
Introduce essays as admission criteria based on Sedlacek's non-cognitive predictors of success.	Redesign orientation programs to clearly emphasize importance of academic progress in first year.	Create Office for Academic Advising Support to guide students who have not yet declared a major or are exploring new academic options.	Launch e-portfolios in all first-year writing courses to fully engage students in reflections on their learning outcomes.
Pilot "test-optional admission" for freshmen in order to focus on more retention-relevant admission criteria.	Create online Academic Progress Report and increase expectations for faculty to give early feedback on students' progress in first quarter.	Create Financial Fitness, a program to assist students in the process of managing their personal financial resources while enrolled in college.	Increase academic rigor and quality instruction through expanded faculty development programs and initiatives, such as the DePaul Online Teaching Series.
Partner with Chicago Public Schools' International Baccalaureate programs to increase first-generation college students with particularly high retention likelihood.	Introduce requirement for all freshmen to have laptop computers to enable them to begin their math sequence immediately.	Launch new comprehensive classroom and course scheduling system to improve the capacity to offer the right courses, at the right time, in the right place to meet student demand and optimize classroom use.	Expand programs for students of color, including the STARS Program and Men of Color Initiative, to ensure all students engage fully in the academic and multicultural opportunities at DePaul.
Create DePaul Admission Partnership Program (DAPP) as alternative pathway for students lacking the academic or financial profile for direct admission.	Create degree audit systems and online Degree Progress Report for students, advisors, and faculty to better map and manage students' academic progress toward degree.		
Increase applicant demand for freshman class through Common Application and expanded marketing.			

Table 10.4. Key Measures Related to DePaul University's Student Retention Strategy

Profile	Progress	Process	Promise
Goal: Elevate the academic profile of entering student classes while keeping a mission-balanced financial and demographic mix.	*Goal: Ensure students' initial academic success and continuous academic progress toward a DePaul degree.*	*Goal: Improve and integrate all processes and services related to students' enrollment at DePaul.*	*Goal: Ensure all students' expectations and experiences are consistent with the promise of DePaul's mission and brand.*
Freshman application/admit rates	Satisfactory academic progress in first quarter and first year	Transaction metrics in all core student services (e.g., traffic patterns in service centers, presenting concerns, metrics of satisfactory problem resolution)	Student surveys regarding expectations and experiences (e.g., NSSE, Graduating Student Survey, Alumni Survey)
Enrollment of first-generation, low-income, and minority students compared with peer institutions	Tracking of student progress over time toward degree	Registration or financial holds, blocked registrations, withdrawal, and leave-of-absence patterns	Brand research and market studies of DePaul's position and perceived brand attributes
Academic profile of freshman class	Time-to-degree metrics	Student satisfaction surveys focused on advising, services, and campus experiences	Assessment of learning outcomes through academic program review
Comparative market position	Levels of math placement at matriculation		Percentage of students participating in research, service learning, study abroad, and other high-impact experiences
Chicago/Chicago Public Schools enrollments	DFW rates in gateway courses		Career placement outcomes and graduate school enrollment patterns
Retention/graduation rates compared with predicted rates	Registration and course-taking patterns		Participation of Chicago regional employers and alumni mentors with career programs
Efficacy of non-traditional admission variables in predicting student success			Alumni affinity measures
Landing rates and destinations for students transferring out of DePaul			

understanding of retention issues among various campus constituencies, structured the group's research agenda, set University retention goals, and managed retention-focused initiatives. The 4 Ps have been instrumental in galvanizing institution-wide attention to retention and moving forward with a comprehensive approach to institutional improvement.

References

College Board. 2011. *How Four-Year Colleges and Universities Organize Themselves to Promote Student Persistence: The Emerging National Picture*. New York: The College Board Advocacy & Policy Center.

Kalsbeek, D. H. 2007. "Reflections on Strategic Enrollment Management Structures and Strategies." *College and University Journal* 82(3):3–9.

Kalsbeek, D. H. 2008, November. "When You Wish Upon a Czar and Other Observations on Student Retention Strategies." Paper presented at the AACRAO SEM XVIII Conference, Los Angeles.

Seidman, A. 2012. *College Student Retention: Formula for Student Success*. Lanham, Md.: Rowman & Littlefield Publishers, Inc.

DAVID H. KALSBEEK *is the senior vice president for the division of Enrollment Management and Marketing at DePaul University.*

INDEX

HE 160   Codes of Conduct in Academia

John M. Braxton, Nathaniel J. Bray
Chapters of this issue of New Directions for Higher Education present
tenets of codes of conduct for the presidency, academic deans,
admissions officers, fund-raising professionals, faculty who teach
undergraduate students, and faculty who teach graduate students. The
need for such codes of conduct stems from the client-serving role of
colleges and universities. Such clients include prospective donors,
prospective students and their families, the individual college or
university, faculty members, undergraduate and graduate students, and
the knowledge base of the various academic disciplines. Because
presidents, academic deans, admissions officers, fund-raising
professionals, and faculty members experience role ambiguity and
substantial autonomy in the performance of their roles, codes of
conduct are needed to protect the welfare of the clients served. The
authors offer recommendations for policy and practice regarding the
proposed codes of conduct. Organizational constraints and
possibilities of enacting such codes are also discussed.
ISBN: 978-1-1185-3775-6

**HE 159   In Transition: Adult Higher Education Governance
in Private Institutions**

J. Richard Ellis, Stephen D. Holtrop
Adult degree programs can pose challenges to traditional campus
structures. This volume of case studies shows a number of small,
independent universities addressing various administrative and service
functions for their adult programs. Institutions have unique internal
structures and distinctive histories, which mean some adult programs
remain very connected to the central campus administrative and
service functions while others develop autonomy in a number of areas.
As an adult program grows, its relationship with the traditional
program changes, while outside forces and internal reevaluation of
priorities and finances also work to realign the balance of centralized
and autonomous functions. Balancing these functions in an
institution-specific hybrid structure can provide both a measure of
autonomy and centralized efficiency and consistency. In the end, each
institution needs to find its own balance of centralized and
decentralized services and administrative functions. Mutual
appreciation and collaboration are keys to finding such an institutional
balance.
ISBN: 978-1-1184-7749-6

**HE 158   Dual Enrollment: Strategies, Outcomes, and Lessons for
School–College Partnerships**

Eric Hofmann, Daniel Voloch
In order to achieve the ambitious national goal of increasing the
number of college graduates over the next decade, high schools and
postsecondary institutions must collaborate more intentionally to help
students become college ready. This volume focuses on the goals,

practices, policies, and outcomes of programs that enroll high school students in college courses for college credit. Referred to as dual enrollment programs, these opportunities support students' transition to, and success in, college.

This volume of *New Directions for Higher Education* presents quantitative and qualitative studies that investigate the impact of dual enrollment programs on student and faculty participants. Accounts by dual enrollment program administrators provide examples of how their programs operate and how data have been used to set benchmarks for program success. Chapters also explore models that build off dual enrollment's philosophy of school–college partnerships and embrace a more robust framework for supporting college transition, including the development of early colleges and a new approach to community college design in New York City.

Dual enrollment inhabits a place where practitioners confront significant questions with regard to higher education on a seemingly daily basis. The collection of researchers and practitioners gathered here examine the details of dual enrollment programs, their impact on student achievement and institutional practices, and the role of higher education in improving K–12 education.
ISBN: 978-1-1184-0523-9

HE 157   Peer Leadership in Higher Education

Jennifer R. Keup

Peers have always been an important influence on students' college experience, thereby leading higher education to formalized peer involvement and support that can harness the ubiquitous nature and positive potential of student-to-student interactions. Although early student leadership opportunities were primarily social in focus and the sole province of student affairs, peer leadership is now present in both the academic and cocurricular spheres of the undergraduate experience, covers a wide range of cognitive and affective topics and techniques, and engages a large number of campus constituencies. Peer leadership programs are not only pervasive but also offer an effective and efficient means to advance students' adjustment, learning, development, and success. Student leaders, educators, and paraprofessionals make it financially feasible to run large-scale programs and are likely to be an even greater component of campus life and academic support in the future. The student outcomes of peer leadership are mutually beneficial: the students who provide the mentorship, leadership, or education gain as much, if not more, from the experience than the students they serve. Further, the range of positive gains from peer leadership has significant overlap with personal, civic, and social outcomes of college that are essential for success in a global society and economy. Therefore, it is quite likely that peer leadership is an emerging high-impact practice in support of 21st Century Learning Outcomes, an assertion that finds support in the content of this volume.
ISBN: 978-1-1182-8818-4

HE 156   Changing Course: Reinventing Colleges, Avoiding Closure

Alice W. Brown, Sandra L. Ballard

Institutions of higher education are constantly facing economic challenges to their survival. Nowhere are the challenges greater than in small private colleges and universities across America.

The principal editor of this collection of essays spent twenty-five years as the director of a consortium of more than thirty private colleges in five states. Her experiences in working with college presidents on these ~mpuses and others led her to consider the big question of what makes the difference between a college that closes and one that nearly closes but manages to remain open.

This collection contains stories of colleges in crisis, told mostly by college presidents. Some colleges found no way out, and their stories offer lessons to be learned just as valuable as the stories of colleges that reinvented themselves and survived. No college can assume that its stability is assured in perpetuity. No thriving college is immune from unforeseen disaster, just as no struggling college is irreversibly destined for closure. This issue of *New Directions in Higher Education* offers a range of revealing, hard-won experiences of college presidents who led their campuses in times of crises.
ISBN: 978-1-1182-7433-0

HE 155   Multinational Colleges and Universities: Leading, Governing, and Managing International Branch Campuses

Jason E. Lane, Kevin Kinser
In the past ten years, universities from around the world have been expanding their global reach by creating outposts in multiple countries. The most significant manifestation of this phenomenon is the creation of international branch campuses (IBCs), where students can attend classes, engage in student activities, and earn a degree from the home institution without ever actually visiting the institution's home country.

Because IBCs fall outside of traditional institutional associations and operate in dislocated geopolitical regions, there are few opportunities for faculty and administrators of these entities to discuss common challenges and opportunities. This volume brings together researchers and experienced administrators to provide a scholarly overview and practical reflection about this growing and still volatile subsection of higher education.

The objective of this volume is to address issues of leadership, administration, and governance of branch campuses by using scholarly fieldwork and selected institutional case studies. In exploring the internal and external dynamics of IBCs, this volume includes chapters that address three broad themes: practical administrative strategies; student and academic issues; and institutional environments, cultures, and policy arenas. The volume is important for various audiences, including higher education administrators and faculty and staff living and working in the IBC environment.
ISBN: 978-1-1181-5925-5

HE 154   Disability and Campus Dynamics

Wendy S. Harbour, Joseph W. Madaus
As each wave of students with disabilities breaks ground in higher education, colleges and universities adjust accordingly, with the federal government mandating better access and services through legislation. Administrators and faculty are now seeing a new generation of people with disabilities on campus—they arrive in higher education with knowledge that the law is on their side, ready to learn or work on any campus that is right for them, whether or not the campus itself is ready.
ISBN: 978-1-1181-3402-3

NEW DIRECTIONS FOR HIGHER EDUCATION

ORDER FORM SUBSCRIPTION AND SINGLE ISSUES

DISCOUNTED BACK ISSUES:

Use this form to receive 20% off all back issues of *New Directions for Higher Education*.
All single issues priced at **$23.20** (normally $29.00)

TITLE	ISSUE NO.	ISBN

*Call 888-378-2537 or see mailing instructions below. When calling, mention the promotional code JBNND
to receive your discount. For a complete list of issues, please visit www.josseybass.com/go/ndhe*

SUBSCRIPTIONS: (1 YEAR, 4 ISSUES)

☐ New Order   ☐ Renewal

U.S.	☐ Individual: $89	☐ Institutional: $292
CANADA/MEXICO	☐ Individual: $89	☐ Institutional: $332
ALL OTHERS	☐ Individual: $113	☐ Institutional: $366

*Call 888-378-2537 or see mailing and pricing instructions below.
Online subscriptions are available at www.onlinelibrary.wiley.com*

ORDER TOTALS:

Issue / Subscription Amount: $ _____

Shipping Amount: $ _____
(for single issues only – subscription prices include shipping)

Total Amount: $ _____

SHIPPING CHARGES:

First Item $6.00
Each Add'l Item $2.00

*(No sales tax for U.S. subscriptions. Canadian residents, add GST for subscription orders. Individual rate subscriptions must
be paid by personal check or credit card. Individual rate subscriptions may not be resold as library copies.)*

BILLING & SHIPPING INFORMATION:

☐ **PAYMENT ENCLOSED:** *(U.S. check or money order only. All payments must be in U.S. dollars.)*

☐ **CREDIT CARD:** ☐ VISA ☐ MC ☐ AMEX

Card number _____ Exp. Date _____

Card Holder Name _____ Card Issue # _____

Signature _____ Day Phone _____

☐ **BILL ME:** *(U.S. institutional orders only. Purchase order required.)*

Purchase order # _____
          Federal Tax ID 13559302 • GST 89102-8052

Name _____

Address _____

Phone _____ E-mail _____

Copy or detach page and send to: **John Wiley & Sons, One Montgomery Street, Suite 1200,
San Francisco, CA 94104-4594**

Order Form can also be faxed to: **888-481-2665**

PROMO JBNND